Group Approach to Drama 3

Second edition

David Adland

Longman

LONGMAN GROUP LIMITED
Longman House
Burnt Mill, Harlow, Essex, CM20 2JE, England

First edition © David Adland 1965
This edition © Longman Group Limited 1981

First published 1965
Second edition 1981
ISBN 0 582 21962 0

Set in 11/13 pt Compugraphic Baskerville
by Richard Clay (S.E.Asia) Pte Ltd.

Printed in Singapore by
Selector Printing Co Pte Ltd

Contents

Pair plays

1   Big act

Players	Two players in a show I — a very experienced player You — a young, nervous beginner
Place	A dressing room near the stage on the first night of the show — a variety show with all kinds of acts. The two main players dress as clowns for a comedy double-act. (See 'The stage show' below.)
Other players	Though not essential, other players can dress, make-up, rehearse and simply fill in the time until they go on stage, as a background to the action of this play. Control the action and talking of any background playing so that it does not interfere with the main action.
The stage show	Suggest the show in progress with taped music and applause. Select music for the comic entrance and exit of the two main players. Instead of clowns, pairs can choose to play other acts such as magician and partner, jugglers, acrobats, dancers and so on.
Action	I know you're anxious, you've told me so a dozen times. There's nothing, absolutely nothing to worry about. OK? OK. You'll be great, I'm on with you, we're working together, I'll make sure you're OK. You can depend on me.

You start putting on your clown's costume. That looks fine, really good. I watch you begin your make-up — listen! Sounds like the opening number's going down well. Could be a good audience. If we've got a good audience we'll have them falling about. I go off to watch the show for a moment, just to get the feel of things.

When I come back I can see you're in a state: you're sweating and making a mess of your make-up. I clean it off for you and put a towel round your neck to keep your costume clean. I offer to make you up but you want to do it yourself. I go off back-stage to check that all our comedy props are placed ready.

I find the collapsible chair but the rubber umbrella's missing. No one's seen it — we'll be on soon — we've got to find it! I rush back and search the dressing room frantically. Then I notice you.

3

You are sitting there in front of the mirror, frozen with fear. Your eyes are a mess with smeared make-up and there's a red mark on your collar. All right, all right, in a minute, I'll give you a hand – I've got to find this blasted umbrella! Don't panic, that's all.

You tell me where you put the umbrella for safety. Thanks . . . thanks, that's one problem solved. I clean the mess off your face, get you a fresh collar, fix your make-up myself. Done. I'm rushing round like a maniac and my head is splitting. You look fine.

It's nice to see you sitting back swigging at a bottle while I put on my costume and hunt for my clown shoes and dab at my face with the make-up. Hey – listen! That's the act before us, they're on now. Are you ready? Sure? Before we go out I remember I didn't remember to get some long laces for these stupid clown shoes. I tie about a million knots in what's left of the old laces and pray.

The two players leave as their entrance music starts. Then, as the music is repeated after a short pause, the players return hot and flushed. The comedy act could be shown here, but is probably better kept as an 'off-stage' action. See Playlines.

Thank God that's over! What a mess – oh. I slump down while you do a merry dance round the room and fling yourself into a chair. I pass you the bottle. It was great, you say, great! And you thank me for all my help. Thanks. And *you* were fine, really fine.

I told you there'd be nothing to worry about. Hell!

Playlines
- Improvise the on-stage comedy act for these two players. Props and costume need not be the same as in the play.
- Group play: *First night*. As well as actors for the show, cast the stage manager, lighting technician, wardrobe mistress and make-up. Show the tension increasing as the actors and technicians prepare and the audience arrives. There's trouble with the lights, someone is missing, a costume is wrong and the start is delayed. Everyone is full of nerves and easily upset – though a few seem hardly affected at all. At last the show starts with whispered best wishes to acts going on and awkward silence or congratulations when they come off. The show ends with a

mixture of relief and mutual congratulations; and, as the players and technicians leave, the cleaners arrive.

Viewpoint
- What is the second player (You) so anxious about?
- Have you ever had 'first-night nerves'? How did you overcome them?
- What signs are there that the first player (I) is not as calm and prepared as he or she wants the second player to believe?
- Why doesn't the first player like the second player very much?
- How would you describe the character of the first player?
- Have you ever been in the position of trying to help someone who is near to panic? What did you do? How did *you* feel?
- Discuss how the title 'Big act' has more than one meaning.

Writing
- The second player (the beginner) is one of the hits of the show. A reporter comes backstage to interview him or her. Write the report of this interview, perhaps also reviewing some of the other − less successful − acts and players in the show.
- *Never again.* Later that night a rather drunk first player tells a sympathetic friend about the show − and about that nervous newcomer.
- A comedy sketch. Write the dialogue and/or actions for the stage act of these two players. Their props and costume are mentioned in the play.

2 Inside

Players	Two I – angry, bitter, sad, and afraid You – my friend, my enemy, trying to 'reach' me
Place	A room with three chairs. Two are near each other in a corner; the third is across the room, opposite.
Music	Select music to suggest the strong personal feelings inside each player. This is played *above* the speech level of the players throughout the play. The music should be allowed to make most of the talking inaudible to any audience and be strong enough to guide the players.
Speech	Players should not try to mime their feelings with the help of the music. Finding the right words for your thoughts and feelings will help you both to get 'inside' the experience of these two people.
Action	I walk quickly away from you feeling bitter, feeling sad. I thought you understood, I thought I could trust you. I can trust no one. You stand there, calling after me, wanting me to come back. I do not hear you.

I must build a strong – a *stronger* wall around myself. I walk up and down and then round and round planning and thinking it out, considering my defences. No enemy will ever get near me. No one. I will live alone inside my fortress. I will not be hurt again.

I sit in the corner, secure, happy. I am smiling: I can feel my face smiling. I can almost see the firm wall protecting me. I can, if I want, take a look out of my windows. I see you come into the room, looking for me. Why do I feel afraid?

You see . . . someone you knew. You see a physical knot: arms crossed over my chest, fingers gripping hard, legs drawn back, head hunched down. You think that I am afraid, but I fear no enemies within my castle. Here I am safe.

You hesitate, and sit far away, opposite me. You try to send me a smile that's not real. You know you can't reach me. I remain still, motionless, my eyes without focus. There is nothing I want to see. Your smile fades coldly.

Without looking, I know you are standing beside me. Your hand touches my shoulder lightly, fearfully. I do not mind. And you sit quietly beside me, talking softly, hesitantly, murmuring apologies, saying it doesn't matter, we can forget it, we can talk together, can't we . . .? I don't know what the words say, but I know what you're saying.

My head turns; and I see you smiling at me. I feel happier now. No anger, no bitterness — why this sadness? You are saying something and there is something in your eyes I knew once. What was it?

You stand; move away; return with some final appeal of come on, let's find the others; let's go together, it's all right now. Inside I say yes, yes let's go and I rise and go with you happy and free. But I feel only a kind of sadness.

I see you walk away slowly, hoping I will follow you, call after you. You do not hear me. You turn at the door with a brief sorry smile. There is nothing for you to smile at.

Playlines
- After discussion, prepare a play from the group's experience of feeling 'betrayed' and let down by a friend, parent, employer, teacher or club leader. Your reaction may not be like the one in the play, but attempt to show the inner feelings as well as the external action.
- Use the first two suggestions from Writing, below, for other pair plays or a group play. A group play would show what happens before and after 'Inside'. It could bring in the parents of both players as well as their other, less important friends. A pair could act this as three scenes, perhaps also casting themselves as the parents for another scene.

Viewpoint
- You will either instantly recognise the thoughts and feelings in this play or feel it means nothing to you. In a group discussion, look at your experience of the breakdown of a close relationship which you have relied upon. Have you ever built a 'fortress' for yourself as a protection against other people, against being hurt? Is the withdrawn silence and apparent indifference used as a

7

weapon? Why, when there is a moment of contact and the first player (I) feels happier, can he or she not get up and go with the other person? Is this just a matter of hurt pride — and a desire to hurt back in revenge?

Writing

- Spoken, taped or written story. As the second player (You), tell what has happened between you and the first player *before* the action in this play. You could go on to describe *your* actions and feelings as the second player in the play and say what happened afterwards.
- Spoken or written conversation. This can be in the form of a story, mainly speech, or more directly as a play. You see the action in the play from the parents' point of view. You may not actually see or hear everything that happens, but you learn enough to know that your son's or daughter's relationship with the other person — whether friendship or love — is over. You can choose to be the parents of the first or second player — or a parent of each player.
- Poem: *I know how you feel*.

3   **Unidentified**

Players   Two amateur UFO observers.

Place   A hilltop at night. They are carrying various pieces of equipment such as binoculars, tea-flasks, red flashing lamps and so on.

Script   Base your improvisation on the script or learn parts or all of it.

Action

1 Here we are, then.
YOU Yes.
1 A good clear night.
YOU A bit cold.
1 A bit cold. But lovely and clear.
YOU Yes, it's clear all right.
1 You've brought everything?
YOU Er . . . yes. Might be lucky.
1 Nothing to do with luck.
YOU No.
1 Scientific observation.
YOU Yes.
1 We have a purpose.
YOU Yes?
1 To make contact with *them*.
YOU Another intelligence.
1 Another intelligence. Yes.
YOU Yes.
1 Observations have proved . . .
YOU Yes.
1 *Proved* that they are monitoring us.
YOU Us. Us? You and me?
1 The Earth. Our planet. Whatever they call it. Monitoring every-thing. Everyone.
YOU Why?
1 Why?
YOU Why?
1 That's why we're here. To find out why.
YOU Extra-terrestrial craft.
1 Where? Have you sighted something?

9

YOU No. But it sounds good, doesn't it? Sort of . . . mysterious, out of this world.

I Yes . . . Scan the edge of that cloud, will you?

YOU That cloud?

I That cloud.

YOU Nothing.

I Did you see a flashing red light?

YOU Yes.

I Did you hear a kind of pulsing noise?

YOU Yes.

I Shall we mark it as a sighting?

YOU It was a car. Going over that hill.

I Disappointing. Still . . . soldier on . . .

YOU Yes.

You go off and return in a moment with a box of dominoes and a stick.

YOU Hullo, Earthman.

I What? Oh hullo.

YOU Hullo, Earthman.

I What are you doing with that stick?

YOU This is my coding computer signal aerial. I can receive your messages, Earthman.

I Come off it. You're not another intelligence.

YOU This is my power pack, Earthman.

I That's a box of dominoes.

YOU No, it isn't.

I Yes, it is.

YOU No, it isn't.

I Yes, it is.

YOU I am a visitor from another planet.

I Which one? Which one?

YOU Another planet, far out in deep space, beyond —

I No, you're not.

YOU Yes, I am.

I No, you're not.

YOU Yes, I am.

I Are you doing that humming?

YOU Might be. A little.

I Why are you walking backwards?

YOU I'm not. I'm being drawn backwards . . .

I No, you're not.

YOU . . . by some mysterious kind of force field!

I Is that light behind you anything to do with you?

YOU It's drawing me back – against my will – I am powerless!

I Switch off those lights! I can't see!

YOU They are taking me! Help me, help me . . .

I And good riddance. Never treated UFOs as a serious possibility. Proper observation needs care and patience. We'll make contact sooner or later.

Playlines
- And of course sooner or later the first player (I) does make a sighting and then contact with 'another intelligence'. But perhaps it's not quite what he or she expected.
- Take up this idea of two people totally occupied with (to your way of thinking) some crazy idea or belief that nothing can shake, and build your play around it. Or simply use this play as a starting point for a 'space comedy'.

4 The silent one

Players	Two I — the silent one You — the stranger at the crossroads, strong, angry and violent
Place	A lonely place where two country tracks cross.
Music	Guitar, sitar or Bach.
Action	We meet at crossroads. We each pause to judge which way to go. I am aware that you are watching me. When I turn to follow my path you stand in my way. When I step aside and try to pass you, you leap ahead of me with arms outstretched, grinning fiercely.

I sit down in the dust and open my pack. You watch, growling like an animal, as I fill my cup with water. You spring beside me, knocking the cup from my hands.

I refill the cup from my flask . . . and offer you the water. You jerk away as though there were danger and drop to the ground, watching me. I place the cup between us, and wait. Then you snatch it up, laughing, and drink in great gulps and throw the cup away.

I place bread between us, inviting you to eat with me. You seem puzzled, shaking your head, grunting savagely as you rock to and fro. What trap do you fear? You pounce on the bread and leap away, cramming it triumphantly into your mouth.

I put out the last of my bread, inviting you to share. But you wait, watching me. When I reach out my hand for my share, you thrust it away and eat greedily. A piece drops to the ground. You stare at the piece and then at me. You kick it towards me: I take it and eat.

Now I sit in silence and stillness: you grow restless. You raise your voice against me, abusing me, threatening me. You tip up my pack and trample and scatter my few belongings. I am still and silent. You dance around me laughing, demanding, jeering, showing your fists.

My stillness and silence remain with me. You push me over with your foot and rain blows on me. When you stop, there is blood on my face and pain in my eyes.

I rise and stand before you and you know that I do not fear you. I grip your arm so that you cannot move, though you do not struggle. When I look at you, you return my gaze with difficulty, blinking and turning your head away.

I ask you for water to drink and to bathe my face. You do not move though I release your arm and step back. You are still and silent. Now I am waiting, watching. For the first time you look me directly in the face.

I pick up my flask and shake it: a little water remains. I hold it out to you. You do not move. I push the flask into your hand and you half-raise it to drink. Then you do not move for a long while: until you hold out the flask to me: and I drink.

Playlines
We could meet 'the silent one' in other situations which test his or her 'inner strength'. He or she may overcome not only violence but forms of witchcraft or sorcery or the evil powers of the super-natural. Perhaps there are temptations of various kinds – money, power, success. Show how 'the silent one' struggles against these offers and wins through with 'inner strength'.

Viewpoint
- In what ways is the first player, the silent one, more powerful and commanding than the second?
- Offer your own explanations of the violent behaviour of the second player.
- Explain in your own words what happens between the two players in the final action of the play.
- Describe anyone you know with this kind of 'inner strength'. What impresses you about such people?

Writing
- Story or play: as the second player you return to your friends, perhaps a gang of some kind. You try to explain what happened at the crossroads.
- The whole incident (of the play) is witnessed by the local gossip who fears and hates the violent second player. He or she eagerly reports the story – with colourful detail and exaggeration – to friends in the village.
- Poem: Base this on the theme of the play or on the 'inner strength' of someone you know. Title: *Power*.

5   The Ironshirts are coming!

Players   Two
Grusha, a young woman
Peasant woman

Action   As Grusha rushes into the cottage, the peasant woman is bending over the child's crib.

GRUSHA Hide him. Quick! The Ironshirts are coming! I laid him on your doorstep. But he isn't mine. He's from a good family.

PEASANT WOMAN Who's coming? What Ironshirts?

GRUSHA Don't ask questions. The Ironshirts that are looking for it.

PEASANT WOMAN They've no business in my house. But I must have a little talk with you, it seems.

GRUSHA Take off the fine linen. It'll give us away.

PEASANT WOMAN Linen, my foot! In this house I make the decisions! Why did you abandon it? It's a sin.

GRUSHA (*looking out of the window*) Look, they're coming out from behind those trees! I shouldn't have run away, it made them angry. Oh, what shall I do?

PEASANT WOMAN (*looking out of the window and suddenly starting with fear*) Gracious! Ironshirts!

GRUSHA They're after the baby.

PEASANT WOMAN Suppose they come in!

GRUSHA You mustn't give him to them. Say he's yours.

PEASANT WOMAN Yes.

GRUSHA They'll run him through if you hand him over.

PEASANT WOMAN But suppose they ask for it? The silver for the harvest is in the house.

GRUSHA If you let them have him, they'll run him through, right here in this room! You've got to say he's yours!

Experiments   1 *Discuss*:
what you know about Grusha and the peasant woman;
who the Ironshirts are;
why the Ironshirts are after the baby;
whether the peasant woman will betray Grusha and the baby.

14

2 Character

Play Grusha as a frightened girl in a state of panic. Play the peasant woman as a rather slow, gentle countrywoman – a firm and sensible old dear who behaves as if the Vicar has dropped in for tea. Read aloud – then improvise.

Play Grusha as a fiercely determined young girl who gives orders and expects a sensible response. The old peasant woman dithers dottily and half-deaf, hardly aware of what's going on. Read aloud, then improvise, adding any words you need.

3 Questions

'Don't ask questions,' says Grusha. But that's exactly what the peasant woman does in this improvisation. She wants to know everything about the baby and why the Ironshirts are looking for it. As Grusha, you supply the answers to save the child – but aware that time is running out.

4 Fears and excuses

'The silver for the harvest . . .' The peasant woman is naturally afraid of what the Ironshirts will do if they find the baby in her house. She also seems more interested in saving herself and her property than in saving the baby. Improvise endless excuses and fears for the peasant woman – though she always says, Yes, she will help. Grusha is forced to be reasonable and patient – though she feels more and more anxious as time passes.

Action

PEASANT WOMAN Yes. But what if they don't believe me?

GRUSHA You must be firm.

PEASANT WOMAN They'll burn the roof over our heads.

GRUSHA That's why you must say he's yours. His name's Michael. But I shouldn't have told you.

The peasant woman nods.

GRUSHA Don't nod like that. And don't tremble – they'll notice.

PEASANT WOMAN Yes.

GRUSHA And stop saying yes. I can't stand it. (*She shakes the woman.*) Don't you have any children?

PEASANT WOMAN (*muttering*) He's in the war.

GRUSHA Then maybe *he's* an Ironshirt? Do you want *him* to run children through with a lance? You'd bawl him out: 'No fooling with lances in my house!' you'd shout. 'Is that what I've reared you for? Wash your neck before you speak to your mother!'

PEASANT WOMAN That's true, he couldn't get away with anything around here!

GRUSHA So you'll say he's yours?

PEASANT WOMAN Yes.

GRUSHA Look! They're coming!

There is a knocking on the door. The women don't answer. Enter Ironshirts. The peasant woman bows low. (The Corporal's words can be spoken by Grusha.)

THE CORPORAL Well, here she is. What did I tell you? Lady, I have a question for you.

PEASANT WOMAN (*falling suddenly to her knees*) Soldier, I didn't know a thing about it. Please don't burn the roof over our heads.

THE CORPORAL What are you talking about?

PEASANT WOMAN I had nothing to do with it. She left it on my doorstep, I swear it!

Experiments

1 *Discuss*:
what you *now* know about Grusha and the peasant woman;
why the peasant woman betrays Grusha.

2 *Character*
Play Grusha as a rich, upper-class 'do-gooder' who is rather condescending to the poor, working-class peasant woman. As such, Grusha is not expecting any favours or begging for help: she just naturally expects the silly woman to be sensible and do her duty.

3 *Style*
Play as a bright American TV comedy – where nearly every line expects (and gets) a laugh. Nothing is serious, nothing is meant: only the laugh matters. Your partner can help by laughing as if he or she were the audience. The ending, of course, should be hysterically funny and greeted with wild applause. Improvise very freely.

4 Devise your own ending to the scene, carrying it on as far as you wish. Try working (1) towards a tragic ending, (2) for a comedy ending, (3) for a hopeful ending. You can bring in any other characters that you need.

6 Routine assignment

Players   Two
    Cask
    Andreyevsky

Action   CASK Now. How do you feel like ferreting something out for us in Baluchistan?

ANDREYEVSKY Not another foot-slogging job, I hope. To Khartoum and back.

CASK No. This is something nearer home. And it's going to be a bit of a wild goose chase, I'm afraid, but it can't be helped.

ANDREYEVSKY Interflora?

CASK That's right. It's beginning to look as if they're on to Project Number One Death Trap.

ANDREYEVSKY Which is?

CASK The new dual-purpose concrete-mixer and combine harvester being developed by Tottenham Borough Council for use under the North Sea.

ANDREYEVSKY Aha. So my job is what?

Experiments   1 *Discuss*:
who the two men are;
where this conversation probably takes place;
Project Number One's chances of success.

2 *Character*
Read aloud or improvise this scene, playing a cool, crisp Cask who is quite oblivious of Andreyevsky's fear-crazed panic. What is he afraid of? Is he a double-agent? Is this a trap? You may need to add your own skilful undercover words.

3 *Accent – disguise*
Cask is obviously a thorough English gentleman-spy. It's so obvious it makes you wonder if he's genuine. And Andreyevsky? With a name like that, could he be – Russian? Or Arabian? Or a Tottenham Borough Councillor? Experiment with accents for each, reading aloud the script – or learning it, and then improvising.

4 *The rendezvous*

A secret agent must find an unusual place where a contact can be made without being overheard. For a free improvisation of this scene try a merry-go-round with the horses bobbing up and down, a meter cupboard under the stairs, at a concert with one playing the piano and the other inside it.

5 *The job*

'Aha. So my job is what?' As Cask, provide a job for Andreyevsky in keeping with the style of this scene. End with:

ANDREYEVSKY Good. You seem to have thought of everything.

CASK We like to take as few chances as possible.

Action

CASK Your job will be twofold. In the first place we want you to get yourself fished up on the end of a line off the pier at Brighton under cover of an angling competition, hitch a lift to Doncaster in an ice-cream van, insert a small Black and Decker rotary scythe with hedge-clipper attachment under the dashboard, and lie low.

ANDREYEVSKY And in the second place?

CASK In the second place, and at the same time, we want you to impersonate three six-foot guardsmen in quick succession while playing the bagpipes on the back of a motorbike.

ANDREYEVSKY Bagpipes? On the back of a motorbike? No, thank you. I've had all the bagpipes I want. In Swansea.

CASK Yes – well, I'm not pushing them, if you'd sooner chance your arm with something else. What do *you* suggest?

ANDREYEVSKY If it were left to me, I think I'd sooner settle for the 1923 Sheraton-type twin-action harpsichord, frankly.

CASK The good old standby.

ANDREYEVSKY People sneer at it, but it's reliable, and it's easy to ditch if you have to.

CASK True enough. Oh, and . . . I don't suppose you'll find yourself with time on your hands, but in case you do you might like to know that we've got someone on either side of the road from Torquay to Headingley with four spare sets of Winsor and Newton's Number Nine lino-cut tools.

ANDREYEVSKY Good. You seem to have thought of everything.

CASK We like to take as few chances as possible.

Experiments

1 *Discuss*:
Andreyevsky's chances of success;
what Cask hasn't thought of.

2 *Character*
The 'job', as always, is urgent — success vital. Cask is responsible, and beginning to crack under the strain. Andreyevsky's easy casualness enrages Cask and sends his blood-pressure soaring. Read aloud or improvise this scene and then continue it to the point of Cask's total collapse.

3 *Blowing your cover*
Defy any attempt to be overheard by arming yourselves with any two brass band instruments and playing the 'Colonel Bogey' march. Hold your conversation — reading aloud or improvising — between puffs and during your musical 'rests'. Avoid practising beforehand as this is likely to draw attention to you. Complete this mission despite threats and appeals to your better nature. (Less talented spies may select their own instruments and music.)

4 *Counter-action: group of four or more*
As this scene ends, Cask and Andreyevsky realise that their plans have been overheard by two counter-spies who are there in disguise. The disguise is, of course, superb, astonishingly imaginative and finally — unsuccessful. Decisive action is called for.

5 *A secret conversation: group of four or more*
This vital conversation is interrupted by other players who appear as waiters, lift attendants, lost children, old age pensioners in invalid chairs, blood donors, District Nurses, autograph hunters, railway modellers, While-You-Wait Shoe Repair specialists *and* counter-spies — in disguise, of course. Keep the whole thing going and complete your secret conversation: it's for your country, after all.

7   The instructions

Players	Two Ben Gus
Action	BEN Time's getting on. GUS I don't like doing a job on an empty stomach. BEN (*wearily*) Be quiet a minute. Let me give you your instructions. GUS What for? We always do it the same way, don't we? BEN Let me give you your instructions. Gus sighs and goes and sits next to Ben. BEN When we get the call, you go over and stand behind the door. GUS Stand behind the door. BEN If there's a knock you don't answer it. GUS If there's a knock on the door I don't answer it. BEN But there won't be a knock on the door. GUS So I won't answer it.
Experiments	1 *Discuss*: what the instructions are leading up to; what kind of 'call' they might get; what you know about the two men. 2 *Tension* Read the script aloud, playing Ben in a forceful, urgent way, and Gus in a slow, stupid way. Aim at creating a sense of danger and anxious preparation. 　　After playing as above, improvise the same scene, adding any dialogue of your own that you want. 3 *Character* Read aloud or improvise this scene, playing Ben and Gus as two elderly spinsters: Ben is sharp and bossy, Gus is nervous and childishly obstinate. 　　Read aloud or improvise this scene with Ben and Gus as countrymen in a village pub – with Gus a little drunk.

4 *Style*

Improvise this scene freely, adding or changing as much dialogue as you like, in the style of a music hall comedy act. Use a loud, brash, knockabout manner – 'I say, I say, I say, time's getting on' – 'I know it is, I'm hungry' – 'Don't tell me, don't tell me, you're always hungry' –.

Improvise this scene in the style of a hard-bitten gangster film or of a tough Western, adding dialogue of your own.

Action

BEN When the bloke comes in –
GUS When the bloke comes in –
BEN Shut the door behind him.
GUS Shut the door behind him.
BEN Without divulging your presence.
GUS Without divulging my presence.
BEN He'll see me and come towards me.
GUS He'll see you and come towards you.
BEN He won't see you.
GUS (*absently*) Eh?
BEN He won't see you.
GUS He won't see me.
BEN But he'll see me.
GUS He'll see you.
BEN He won't know you're there.
GUS He won't know you're there.
BEN He won't know *you're* there.
GUS He won't know I'm here.
BEN I take out my gun.
GUS You take out your gun.
BEN He stops in his tracks.
GUS He stops in his tracks.
BEN If he turns round –
GUS If he turns round –
BEN You're there.
GUS I'm here.

Experiments

1 *Character*

Read aloud or improvise this script, with Ben getting angrier and angrier, and Gus more and more confused.

2 *Change of mood*

It's all a great joke to Gus, who laughs as he repeats Ben's words and rehearses what he must do. Then suddenly it's not funny any more when they reach Ben's line: 'I take out my gun.' As Gus moves and repeats 'He stops in his tracks' and 'If he turns round', he realises that *he* could be the target. He stands terrified at the end as he repeats, 'I'm here.'

3 *Character*

Continue the earlier work as two elderly spinsters. Gus becomes more frightened and hysterical, Ben more commanding and threatening.

4 *Giving instructions*

Use the style of this play to give your own instructions to your partner. You might be a foreman and a labourer on a building site; an elderly vicar and an earnest young curate about to take his first church service; a male police sergeant and a rather pretty policewoman; a shopper giving directions to a foreign motorist; a doctor instructing a trainee nurse in the treatment of a unconscious patient.

5 *Action*

There *is* a knock at the door. Improvise the reactions of Gus and Ben, bringing in other players if you need them.

8 Attempt the impossible

Players   Two
                      Joan
                      Her mother – also plays Archangel Michael and Joan's brother.

Action   Joan is sobbing after being punished by her father.

MOTHER Now, now, now, you don't have to upset yourself. You remember when you were little, we would rock away your nightmares together . . . Who is it, Joan? You can tell your mother. Don't you even know his name, perhaps? Why, your father might even agree to him; he's not against a good marriage for you.

JOAN It isn't marriage that I have to think of, mother. The blessed St Michael has told me I should leave the village, put on man's clothes, and go and find his Highness the Dauphin, to save the realm of France.

MOTHER Joan, I speak nicely and gently to you, but I won't have you talking wickedness. And I won't have you put on man's clothes, not if you beg at my grave. Have my daughter a man! You let me catch you, my goodness!

JOAN But mother, I should have to, if I'm to ride a horse with the soldiers.

MOTHER Joan of Arc on a horse! It would be the talk of the village. Such grand ideas, indeed!

JOAN But if I don't ride a horse, how can I lead the soldiers?

MOTHER And you won't go with the soldiers, either, you wicked girl! I'd rather see you cold and dead. A daughter spins, and scrubs, and stays at home. Your grandmother never left this village, and neither have I, and neither will you, and when you have a daughter of your own, neither will she. Do you want to kill me?

JOAN No, mother!

MOTHER You do: I can see you do. And you'll destroy yourself in the end if you don't soon get these thoughts out of your head. (*She goes.*)

Experiments

1 *Discuss*:
what Joan wants to do;
why her mother won't let her;
'a daughter spins, and scrubs, and stays at home'.

2 Play Joan as an impatient, headstrong schoolgirl who demands her own way in everything. Her mother is scolding and cross: she will stand for no nonsense like this. Read aloud – then improvise.

Play Joan as a delightfully imaginative child who teases her mother with her wonderful fancies. Her mother plays up to her, knowing it's all a game – but sometimes Joan's 'make-believe' becomes too real and worrying. Read aloud – then improvise, adding words of your own.

3 *Style*
Improvise freely in the broad comic style of a pantomime like *Cinderella*. The mother is the long-suffering 'Dame' (traditionally a man dressed as a woman) who plays to the audience for big laughs with her comic 'business' with her dress, hair and walk. Joan is a young and innocent 'Cinders' who tries to hold the old dear's attention and get her to understand.

4 *'Your grandmother never left this village . . .'*
And she, too, has something to say to Joan about her mad ideas – a long, rambling word about her proper duties as a daughter – and no wicked talk about soldiers. Joan's protests are swept aside by this elderly flood.

Action

JOAN You see, holy St Michael, it isn't possible; they won't ever understand. No one will. It is better that I should give up at once. Our Lord has said that we have to obey our father and mother.

THE ARCHANGEL (*played by mother*) But first, Joan, you have to obey God.

JOAN But if God commands the impossible?

THE ARCHANGEL Then you have to attempt the impossible, calmly and quietly. He doesn't ask the impossible of everybody, but He does ask it of you. That is all.

JOAN Well, I will go. All right, then. It's all decided. I shall go and find my uncle Durand. With him I always get my own way. He's as easy to manage as a tame sparrow. I shall kiss him on both cheeks, and on the top of his head, and sit on his lap, and he will say 'Oh Lord, Oh Lord', and take me to Vaucouleurs!

BROTHER (*played by mother*) You're a silly donkey! Why did you have to go and tell the old people all that stuff? Next time, if you give me a ha'penny, I won't say a word about where I saw you.

JOAN Oh, it was you who told them, you beastly little pig? Sneak, sneak, I'll give you a tweak! Tell tales out of school, duck him in a muddy pool! There's your halfpenny, lardy-head. Tell-tale-tit, your tongue shall split, and all the children in the town shall have a little bit!

Experiments

1 *Character*

Play the Archangel slowly and quietly, using a whisper-voice so that it seems like Joan's thoughts being spoken aloud.

Once Joan has made her decision – 'Well, I will go', she is a little girl again, teasing and name-calling and chasing her brother. Read aloud – then improvise.

2 *Sneak, sneak . . .*

Her brother delights in telling his mother what Joan's been up to – and what she plans to do now. Why should he care if he gets her into trouble: she's so stupid to think she could dress up like a soldier – as if a girl could fight! And she's too mean to pay him to keep quiet. Serves her right!

3 *Attempt the impossible*

St Michael the Archangel reports back to St Peter. St Michael is gloomy: Joan seems such a silly, thoughtless girl – she's no idea of what she's letting herself in for. St Peter reassures him like a kind, wise uncle: Joan *is* special: in her heart she believes and knows. After all, he should know better than to judge by appearances: has he forgotten about a baby who was born in a cattle shed?

4 *A tame sparrow*

Uncle Durand is not quite so easy to manage – and he has plenty of questions to ask about Joan's mission. In the end, of course, Joan charms and flatters him so delightfully that he can't refuse her, despite his misgivings.

9   Murder

Players
: Two
: Macbeth, a General
: Lady Macbeth

Action

LADY MACBETH I laid their daggers ready;
  He could not miss them. Had he not resembled
  My father as he slept, I had done't.

Macbeth comes in carrying two bloodstained daggers.

LADY MACBETH My husband!

MACBETH I have done the deed. Didst thou not hear a noise?

LADY MACBETH I heard the owl scream and the crickets cry.
  Did not you speak?

MACBETH When?

LADY MACBETH Now.

MACBETH As I descended?

LADY MACBETH Ay.

MACBETH Hark!
  Who lies i' the second chamber?

LADY MACBETH Donalbain.

MACBETH (*looking at his hands*) This is a sorry sight.

LADY MACBETH A foolish thought, to say a sorry sight.

MACBETH One cried 'God bless us!' and 'Amen' the other,
  As they had seen me with these hangman's hands.
  I could not say 'Amen'
  When they did say 'God bless us!'

LADY MACBETH Consider it not so deeply.

MACBETH But wherefore could not I pronounce 'Amen'?
  I had most need of blessing, and 'Amen'
  Stuck in my throat.

LADY MACBETH These deeds must not be thought
  After these ways; so, it will make us mad.

Experi-
ments
: 1 *Discuss*:
: what has happened;
: how each character feels

2 Read the scene aloud in whispers, whether the character is alone or not. Use the whisper-voice to suggest night and the atmosphere of murder and fear. Some words and phrases, especially in the final two speeches, can be selected for much greater volume and emphasis.

3 Crazy old Macbeth is having a bad day – even for him. Here he is trotting about in the middle of the night with a couple of kitchen knives. The best policy for his wife, as always, is to humour him. Read through, then improvise from 'I have done the deed'.

4 *Sculpture – a physical picture*
Help each other to create a physical picture using the whole body and face for each of the following moments in the play. Both players should hold or 'freeze' the position for a silent count of five. The dialogue need not be spoken.
(a) LADY MACBETH My husband!
  MACBETH I have done the deed.
(b) MACBETH Hark!
    Who lies i' the second chamber?
  LADY MACBETH Donalbain.
(c) MACBETH (*looking at his hands*) This is a sorry sight.
  LADY MACBETH A foolish thought, to say a sorry sight.
(d) MACBETH 'Amen'
    Stuck in my throat.
  LADY MACBETH These deeds must not be thought
    After these ways.

5 *Word-chain*
The following speeches are built up from key words in the text. Macbeth and his wife speak at the same time – though not necessarily at the same speed or volume or with the same emphasis. Make your own experiments with these word-chains.
LADY MACBETH Owl. Scream. Cry. Daggers. Father. Husband. Daggers. Deeds. Cry.
MACBETH God bless us. God bless us. God bless us.
LADY MACBETH Make us mad. Make us mad. Make us mad.
MACBETH Amen. Amen. Amen. Amen. Amen.
LADY MACBETH Mad. Mad. Mad. Mad. Mad. Mad. Ma – ma –.
MACBETH Amen. Ame – ame – am – am – a – a –.

Action

LADY MACBETH Go, get some water,
And wash this filthy witness from your hand.
Why did you bring these daggers from the place?
They must lie there. Go, carry them and smear
The sleepy grooms with blood.

MACBETH I'll go no more.
I am afraid to think what I have done;
Look on't again I dare not.

LADY MACBETH Infirm of purpose!
Give me the daggers. The sleeping and the dead
Are but as pictures. 'Tis the eye of childhood
That fears a painted devil.

She goes out with the daggers. Knocking is heard.

MACBETH Whence is that knocking?
How is't with me when every noise appals me?
What hands are here! Ha — they pluck out mine eyes!
Will all great Neptune's ocean wash this blood
Clean from my hand? No . . .

Lady Macbeth returns.

LADY MACBETH My hands are of your colour; but I shame
To wear a heart so white.   (*Knock.*)
I hear a knocking
At the south entry. Retire we to our chamber.
A little water clears us of this deed;
How easy is it then!   (*Knock.*)
Hark! more knocking.
Get on your nightgown, lest occasion call us
And show us to be watchers. Be not lost
So poorly in your thoughts.

MACBETH To know my deed 'twere best not know myself.   (*Knock.*)
Wake Duncan with thy knocking! I would thou couldst!

**Experi-
ments**

1 *Discuss*
Macbeth's reactions to what he's done;
Lady Macbeth's feelings towards her husband.

2 Play Lady Macbeth as a weary housewife who has quite enough
to do without looking after a weak husband who has to be scolded

and given simple instructions like a child.

3 Now, improvise the same playing with the help of the following material.
Lady Macbeth's simple instructions are:
(a) Go and wash the blood off your hands.
(b) Take the daggers back.
(c) Smear the grooms with blood.
(d) Give me the daggers.
(e) Let us return to our room.
(f) Put your nightgown on.

She scolds him about the daggers and spells it out for him: 'They – must – lie – there.' She regards him as a coward with childish fears: 'Infirm of purpose . . .' Again she pours scorn on him when she shows her hands. She's kept *her* nerve and had to finish the job for him. She would be ashamed to be such a coward.

4 *Sculpture – a physical picture*
Help each other to create a physical picture using the whole body and face for each of these moments in the play. The positions should be held for a silent count of five. The dialogue need not be spoken.
(a) Why did you bring these daggers from the place?
(b) Give me the daggers.
(c) Whence is that knocking? (Macbeth only.)
(d) Ha – they pluck out mine eyes! (Macbeth only.)
(e) My hands are of your colour.
(f) A little water clears us of this deed; How easy is it then!
(g) Wake Duncan with thy knocking! I would thou couldst!

5 *Confession*
Interview Macbeth and Lady Macbeth in turn as part of your murder inquiry. Each gives you a precise account of their movements on the night in question and is willing to describe their motives and thoughts. Decide how each regards his or her own actions and those of the other. You can use your own words or Shakespeare's or a mixture of the two. The interview should only cover the events described in the text given here (both parts). It could be extended to previous events if you are familiar with the play, or be created imaginatively.

10   A position of command

This play is one of three texts dealing with power and corruption. The others are a group play, 'Power' (page 47), and a playgame, 'Some of the time' (page 37).

Players   Two

I – waiting, obeying orders

You – in a position of command

Place   A very plain room, carpeted, with one small chair which faces a second, larger chair at the end of the room. A screen could be used to conceal this chair, but appropriate mime is sufficient.

Action   I am sitting here waiting. There is nothing to do, not even a magazine, or a picture on the wall or a pattern on the carpet. I wait.

You are making me wait, I know that. You come in without warning, without looking, without speaking. I half-rise, but you ignore me.

You touch a button on the end wall which slides back to reveal a large chair. You admire the chair and then sit with slow dignity. You look very powerful and commanding to me.

Stand, you say, and I rise immediately. You turn your head slowly and stare at the wall on your left. I wonder if I ought to cough or move forward or – what? I obey your order to sit.

You turn your head slowly and stare at the wall on your right. I don't like to interrupt, but – I wait. I obey your order to stand, to sit, to stand, to sit.

Something has happened to your face: you are smiling! I know you are smiling. At me. At your power. I ignore your order to stand, feeling nervous, feeling I really ought to . . .

There is a pause. You suddenly seem to see *me*, a person, sitting there. You frown, repeat your order, but the authority is gone: I ignore it easily. You try again more forcefully; I feel there is nothing behind the words.

You stand, fierce, shouting orders: sit, stand, sit, stand. You falter and stop when you see me sitting there comfortably, smiling at you.

Playlines
- Repeat the play with a change-over of roles. This will enable each player to experience the 'position of command' and the inferior, obedient position.

  Discuss how you felt playing each of the roles. In which role, for example, did you feel more comfortable and natural? Did you like taking orders as much as giving them? How did you feel when you found you did not have to go on obeying? How did you feel when your orders were no longer obeyed?

- Build up a group play which leads into this situation. Show, for example, how the first player successfully commands other players before failing with this one. Explain what is happening — why this display of power, of absolute authority, is necessary. Decide whether this is some kind of James Bond set-up, a spy-school, a test of the loyalty of terrorists, a present or future dictatorship, a police-state interview of a suspect, or a vist to the Head.

  Change roles for replays of this group play which shows the first player exercising his power successfully. Discuss your feelings after playing each role.

Experiment
Cast *all* the inferior, obedient players either from boys or girls; cast a player of the opposite sex to all the others in the position of command.

Discuss what difference this makes to your feelings. How, for example, do boys like taking orders from a girl? How did a girl feel when giving orders to boys?

Use this form of casting for both the pair play and the group play.

Viewpoint
- How do you feel when you have to wait for someone? How do you feel when you're waiting to see a doctor or dentist, or your Headteacher?
- What makes the second player (You) seem so 'powerful and commanding'?
- Why does the second player not look at the first?
- How do the orders become easy to ignore? How do the feelings

of the first player change as he or she realises that 'there is nothing behind the words'?

- Describe what has happened between the two players by the end of the play.
- Have you ever managed to reverse your feelings in a situation where you began by feeling weak or insecure or inferior?
- Do you know the feeling of being superior to someone else? Are you able to tell others what to do – and get them to do it?

Writing

- As the second player, you dictate a tape or letter after this meeting, offering your resignation from this position of command. You give your reasons but try, unsuccessfully, to conceal the real reasons.
- Poem or story: *Boss*.
- As the first player, you meet a friend outside who feared you were in for a bad time with the second player. He is astonished at the change in your character. Give the conversation between you as a story or play.

Playgames

In a playgame a few specific elements of a play are set in advance.
All the other decisions are made by the players as they go along.
The play develops freely, like a game, different every time.

11 PLAYGAME Identity

Object
: The object of the game is for each player to create his or her own character and then to bring all the characters together, or in contact with one another, during the story.

Characters
: The character you choose may be of either sex, older or younger than you are, historical, from fiction, from film or TV, invented by you, someone known to you, a member of your family.

Action
: Begin by sitting in a circle. There is no preliminary discussion about what characters you may create or what the story is. Suggestions may be made to players who get 'stuck', but choice is free and unlimited — and does not have to take other players' choices of character into consideration.

In turn, each player announces his or her character and offers some description of appearance, age, health, job and so on, as necessary. The rest of the group may ask for any further information until they have a clear picture of the character.

Work round the group until there is a complete set of characters. Some of these characters may be related to one another because there is nothing to prevent a player from declaring any relationship he or she likes with any of the characters announced so far. If someone says he or she is Queen Victoria, a later player may claim to be Prince Albert or John Brown or Disraeli. A player may claim to be related as an aunt, cousin, grandparent to *any* character, whether historical or fictional; he or she may claim to be a friend or neighbour; and of course a player may not 'know' any of the other characters at all.

It is assumed that all the characters are 'alive' whether they are drawn from history, literature, television or elsewhere. Players may choose to be the 'ghost' of some character or arrive mysteriously due to some kind of time machine or time warp.

Someone may be willing to start the story going, or simply work round the group. It is usually better to allow characters to come into the story when they see the right opportunity. The first player may begin in any way. He or she may simply get up, have breakfast (perhaps talking to an imaginary husband or wife) and go to work on the local bus. A 'grandfather' character may stroll to the pub for a pint and a game of darts. 'Aunty' may get all dressed up to see her sister and her children. Hitler orders 'Operation Sealion' – the invasion of England. Neil Armstrong takes one giant step on the moon.

Each of the characters finds a way, an opportunity of linking with one or more of the other characters and of helping to develop the story. The characters do not have to be 'active' all the time: some may appear only briefly, others come and go; while a few are continuously present. The playing characters need to be constantly aware of the whole range of other characters and to make or allow 'openings' for them to enter the story.

The story does not have to be rounded off. The playgame is complete once all the characters have entered the story and carried it forward in some way. As soon as there is a clear story or situation, the group can either proceed to an improvised ending or stop and discuss their work before completing it.

12 Some of the time

This is one of three texts dealing with power and corruption. The others are a pair play; 'Position of command' (page 30), and a group play, 'Power' (page 47).

Play
The play is designed for eight players. It is also an example of how the playgame works.

Players
President
Chancellor
Third Party leader
People – No 1, No 2, No 3, No 4, No 5

Playgame
The 'rules' for the playgame follow the actions of the play.

Props
Paper money or coins from a board game are required for both play and playgame. Allow twenty coins or notes for each of the eight players in the play, and about twice as much for each player in the playgame.

Action
The King is dead! Long live the Republic! The people gather to elect their new President. They shout out the name of the person they want.

The President is elected by a public show of hands. There is only one vote against him or her — that of the Third Party leader. The President moves to a special chair apart from everyone else.

The President is allowed to make his own free choice of Chancellor — he or she is not elected by the people. The President chooses the player cast as Chancellor. He or she sits beside the President and takes charge of all the treasury money.

The President and Chancellor discuss privately what wages should be paid out by the State to everyone. Then they announce the first law: fair and equal wages for all.

The people line up and each receives the same amount of money. The Chancellor takes the same amount. The President receives *twice* this amount.

Most of the people are satisfied with what they receive, though there are the usual small grumbles. The Third Party leader tries to build up this discontent with demands for higher wages. He or she also suggests that the Chancellor could be taking more than his equal share, and that the President gets too much.

Meanwhile the President and Chancellor discuss the level of taxes to be paid to the State by everyone. They announce the second law: fair and equal taxation for all. The President pays no taxes. The people line up to pay their taxes, handing back some of the money they received.

No one likes paying taxes, though they agree that they are necessary. The Third Party leader gains his or her first recruit — No 1 of the people — and the Party becomes more active. They tell the people that taxes are too high, especially as wages are so low. They spread doubts about the Chancellor's honesty. They even hint that the President is weak because he allows his Chancellor to do what he likes.

The President and Chancellor now announce fair and equal higher wages for all. The people receive their money.

Most people are happy and satisfied. They like the President and trust the Chancellor. But some listen to the arguments of the Third Party: they gain their second recruit — No 2 of the people. Now they demand the sacking of the Chancellor.

Out of the original eight players, there are now three people — Nos 3, 4 and 5 — who will vote *for* the ruling President and his Chancellor. The Third Party also has three votes from its leader and two recruits. The Chancellor cannot vote while in office. The President can give a casting vote which must be accepted.

The President asks the people to vote for or against the Chancellor. The voting is split: three people vote for, three Third Party votes against. The President casts his vote to retain his Chancellor.

The President reports the need to re-equip the Army as there is a threat of invasion. To raise the money, higher taxation is announced. The people pay reluctantly. Some wish that they had voted differently.

Now there is increasing opposition and the Third Party gains another member – No 3 of the people. The Party demands the sacking of the Chancellor – or the President's resignation. A quick vote shows the Third Party with a majority of 4–2, and the Chancellor is dismissed.

The President makes his own free choice of a new Chancellor. He chooses No 4 of the people left. The new Chancellor calls in all the money paid out so far. After discussing the matter with the President, he or she announces the first law. The people line up to receive their fair and equal wages.

The Third Party immediately challenges the new wages. They hold protest meetings, they try to turn the people against the new Chancellor by accusing him of corruption, and some refuse to accept any money at all. They try to gain new members by arguments, threats or bribery. No 5 of the people is persuaded to join.

Now only the ex-Chancellor supports the ruling party. A vote of 5–1 brings the dismissal of the second Chancellor. The President's position seems hopeless and he considers resigning. He decides to choose a third Chancellor and try to keep the Third Party out of power. This is his last chance to rule successfully. If the vote goes against his third Chancellor, he himself loses office automatically.

Since the President is not allowed to choose an ex-Chancellor, he is forced to choose from the Third Party. He chooses No 1. The new Chancellor announces high wages for Third Party members and lower wages for non-members. The ex-Chancellor (No 4) hastily joins the Party.

The President and his only supporter (who was his first Chancellor) protest, but they are ignored. The people are paid. The President's supporter refuses to accept any wages. Taxes are announced: low for Third Party members, high for non-members. As the Third Party holds a wide majority, there is no point in calling for a vote to dismiss his third Chancellor, so the President resigns.

The new President is the Third Party leader.

The new leader of the party in opposition to the ruling party is the former President.

The new President chooses his Chancellor, while his supporters celebrate their victory and drink to their future prosperity.

PLAYGAME

Players
Any number above six; between eight and twelve is most successful. Larger numbers can take part when players are experienced in the game.

Power
There are four 'power units' in the game. These are: the President, the Chancellor, the Third Party and the people. Their powers are listed separately below.

Object
Each 'power unit' has an object concerned with power. The President's object is to rule successfully and to remain in office. Ideally he should rule honestly and fairly and for the good of his people.

The Chancellor's object is to serve his President and to remain in office. Ideally he should serve honestly and fairly and for the good of the people.

The Third Party's object is to overthrow the ruling party and to gain office. Ideally it should wish to do this because it believes it can serve the people better and/or because it believes that the ruling party is corrupt.

The people's object is to obtain fair and honest government which rules for the good of all the people.

Action
All the players are cast as 'people'. They begin by electing a President by a majority vote. He or she then chooses any of the people as Chancellor. The Chancellor takes control of the money.

Now any players can name him- or herself as leader of the Third Party, opposing the present ruling party. But this need not be done at this point in the playgame — it can be done after first laws have been announced (when there is something definite to oppose) or at any point in the game, or not at all. Some Presidents and Chancellors will be able to rule successfully. A Third Party will arise if players want it to, and succeed or fail as players wish.

The laws
As shown in the workings of the play, the laws deal with wages paid by the State and taxes paid to it. The laws should be fair and equal wages for all, and fair and equal taxes for all. The play shows how these laws can be put aside by a corrupt government.

The game proceeds with the regular announcement and payment of wages and taxes.

Opposition During the game the Third Party may rise and try to gain enough members to overthrow the ruling party. See notes on the powers of the Third Party.

Ending the game The game can end with the election of a new President, as the play does.

More interestingly, it can follow the fortunes of several Presidents, and end when time runs out.

It is possible, of course, for the first President, with one or more Chancellors, to rule throughout the game.

Powers 1 *Powers of the people*
All the people elect the President by a majority vote, voting by public show of hands.

The people may ask the President to sack his Chancellor, and force him to do so by a majority vote. This voting can occur whenever the people wish it.

The people allow the President three chances to rule successfully by allowing him to select three Chancellors in turn. The people may join any party (such as the Third Party) opposing the ruling party at any time; they may also leave this party at any time.

2 *Powers of the President*
The President has the right of free choice of Chancellor and the right to sack him or her whether he has been asked to do so or not.

He or she has the right to choose three Chancellors in turn. He must sack his Chancellor if a majority of the people vote for his dismissal.

He may resign his office at any time. He loses office automatically if he sacks, or is forced to sack, his third Chancellor. He cannot be voted out of office.

The President can end a tie-vote for and against the Chancellor by a casting vote. He cannot vote on any other occasion.

He delegates all money matters to his Chancellor. They consult together, and though he cannot force the Chancellor to follow his wishes, he can sack him if necessary.

The President must explain to his people why higher taxes are necessary. For this purpose, news must be received that (a) there is a danger of invasion and the Army must be re-equipped, (b) there is a shortage of natural resources so there must be expensive imports of materials, (c) there is an economic crisis, and so on.

3 *Powers of the Chancellor*

The Chancellor is personally chosen by the President. He or she cannot resign. Only the President, by his own wish or because of a majority vote against his Chancellor, can dismiss him.

Under the President's authority, the Chancellor is responsible for handling all the State's money. Each new Chancellor begins with all the State's money, drawing in any money previously paid out.

Each new Chancellor begins afresh by announcing, after discussions with the President, the first law: fair and equal wages for all.

The Chancellor should receive the same wages as the people; only the President receives twice as much. The Chancellor should pay taxes at the same rate as the people; only the President is exempt.

He should hold a balance between being too generous and too harsh. While he should obey the President's wishes, he should advise him of the proper cause of action, as he sees it, when their views differ.

A Chancellor cannot be reappointed by the same President after being dismissed from office. A new President, of course, has an entirely free choice of Chancellor.

The Chancellor cannot vote while he is in office.

4 *Powers of the Third Party*

The Third Party has no special rights. Its members have the same rights as all the 'people'.

The Party may be formed at any time by any number of persons.

It can remove the Chancellor from office only by gaining a majority vote; it cannot use force or threats against the Chancellor – who is not permitted to resign – or against the President.

The Party can remove the President from office by gaining majority votes against three Chancellors: then the President loses office automatically.

Members of the Party can decide for themselves why they oppose the ruling party and how they would rule in office themselves. They do not have to follow the policy of the Third Party as shown in the play.

The Party can try to gain new members by persuasion, bribery, threats and promises. They may also express genuine grievances against a corrupt President and Chancellor. But to gain power they are prepared to spread rumours and lies about a good President and an honest Chancellor. They may accuse them of 'lining their own pockets', especially when there is an increase in taxes.

Corruption   Even without the activities of a Third Party, the government might not rule fairly and honestly. It is then up to the people to use their vote to change things.

Group plays

13   Power

This play is one of three texts dealing with power and corruption. The others are a pair play, 'A position of command' (page 30), and a playgame, 'Some of the time' (page 37).

Players   Seven or more
King or Queen
Minister of State Security
Field Marshal – can also play General
The remaining four players (in cast of seven) as:

Two courtiers ⎤
                ⎬ The common people
Two guards ⎦

⎡ Traitor 1 ⎤ Leader at trial
⎢ Traitor 2 ⎦ Assistant at trial
⎢ Traitor 3 ⎤ Assassin
⎣ Traitor 4 ⎦ Assassin

For any additional players, simply cast separately from the group above.
The word 'King' is used throughout to refer equally to King or Queen.

Place   The castle requires only two large chairs for the King or Queen and the Minister. It is helpful to have something as a sceptre as a symbol of the ruler's authority. There should also be an axe – made of hardboard or plywood. A pile of heavy books, papers and tapes can be used in the open trial.

Action   I, the King, have absolute power; and all obey me. My courtiers, my officials, my people bow low before me, respectful, humble, loyal. I will raise one of you to sit beside me as my Minister of State Security.

I choose you as my Minister, as my eyes and ears for all plottings, to punish all upstarts, to execute all traitors. I choose you because you are loyal and true; and you give me good counsel.

I bring you to sit beside me, I with my sceptre of power, you with your axe of death. My Court comes before us to pay you honour and in their faces I sometimes see envy and malice and secret plottings, but I have no fear.

You mention, secretly, a name; and I am filled with anger that my

Field Marshal should be disloyal. My guards bring him trembling before us, an old man pleading the innocence of his long life in my service. You shake your head. I give a word. It is a command, and you execute my order willingly.

Soon you have other names; and oily words pour into my ear, soothing suspicion and doubt. The heads fall. (*Execute two traitors.*) Other men rise – you call before me a General and he departs smiling at you as Field Marshal Commander of all the Forces.

The common rabble come with cries of outrage and complaint against you, but I dismiss them and call them liars and traitors and give their leaders over to you. (*Execute two traitors.*)

The common rabble utter their protests with increasing vigour, challenging me as a weak, faint-hearted King, afraid of justice, afraid of truth. A strong King, they say, would hold an open trial and test the evidence himself. I give a word: it is a command, and an open trial is held.

The leaders of the common rabble bring me evidence against my Minister: accounts of bribes and blackmail, of meetings, of gifts, of plottings, of treason, of disloyalty. The documents, the witnesses, overwhelm me and I stand confused and amazed. I see you sitting still and silent, waiting for a word.

The common rabble press me on all sides for your death, and I bid them be silent. I sit for a long while . . . and then I give a word and you are banished for ever.

My people praise me as a strong King who strikes off his offending right hand; and the streets they line with flags to honour me. And when I speak to them from my castle they call me down to walk amongst them so that they may honour me.

Absolute, I, the King, walk freely amongst them and see the ugliness behind the waving flags, see the Field Marshal hurry into my castle and know in that moment that my Minister was innocent. I throw this truth in their faces, challenging their disloyalty.

Their raised knives satisfy me though they are raised to kill me. I do not wish to hear their Song of the Republic. While they sing of freedom, others are already in the castle trying out my throne for democratic size.

Viewpoint
- What are your attitudes to authority? Begin by finding how the players felt themselves. How did the King or Queen feel having 'absolute authority'? How did the Minister feel being able to accuse anyone and execute them? How did the 'traitors' feel about being condemned to death without trial – and perhaps innocent as well?
- The people find that they have power too. How do they use it during the play? What do they want?
- Are there countries like this now where the ruler has absolute power? How has that power usually been obtained? How is that power used?
- What kind of power have you got at the moment? What kind of power would you like to have?
- What has your experience of drama taught you? What human qualities seem important to you?
- Describe a play or a film or a TV programme that showed the struggle between an ordinary person and someone with power.
- What other kinds of power are there? Which is the most beneficial, which is the most dangerous?

14   The expert

Players   Four
Mr or Ms Penny, an auditor checking Town Hall accounts
Mr or Miss Greene, a junior clerk in the Town Hall
Mr or Mrs Arkwright, Town Clerk, a forthright Yorkshire character
Mr or Ms Piper, the expert, a Scot
The play is written as if for all male characters, and small alterations will have to be made to the way the characters address each other when females are played.

Place   Badley Town Hall, Yorkshire. It is 11 a.m. in the Town Clerk's office. Mr or Ms Penny works at a desk piled high with thick ledgers showing all the money received and spent by the departments in the Town Hall. His or her job is to check every entry and to find the accounts correct in every detail.

Action   PENNY Now this . . . (he opens another ledger) . . . is the account for the year 1981–2. Good.
GREENE Everything all right, sir?
PENNY Um? Yes, yes . . . so far . . . very good. (Looking up.) All the figures check, as they should.
GREENE We're very thorough, Mr Penny.
PENNY Of course, of course you must be. Figures are not just figures: they're money.
GREENE (afraid he's going to get a lecture) Oh . . . yes.
PENNY (seeing the chance of giving a lecture) Yes, indeed, young man. Money coming in . . . money going out. Simple, isn't it?
GREENE If you say so, sir. Er – I think I must – (he starts for the door)
PENNY Except for one thing. One thing, hmm? Now I think you could learn a thing or two here, young man, from an expert, like myself.
GREENE (looking round wildly for escape) Yes, I could – thank you, sir. I'll get some more coffee, sir.
PENNY (severely) First things first. Now look at this – (he indicates the open ledger) – here we see money coming in . . . rates, interest on

50

properties, allotment fees, investments and so forth. And over here, in this column, money *out* . . . repairs to vandalised bus shelters, cleansing of all public conveniences, the maintenance of the mayor's Rolls Royce . . . All very proper. You see my point?

GREENE (*confused*) Er yes, sir, er no, not quite, I think . . . .

PENNY Yes, you need the trained, expert eye of course. Not just to *look*, but to *ask*. Yes! To ask the key question when money goes *out*. Eh? And that question is —?

GREENE (*desperately*) Who's taken it?

PENNY (*aghast*) No! Certainly not! Rather — has the money been spent properly? You see! Has it, so to speak, been spent *wisely*? Ah . . .!

GREENE Ah . . .!

PENNY Good man! Here we have: 'To cleaning Town Hall windows — one hundred pounds.' Now — our question. And we must answer, mustn't we, that since the Town Hall officials must have ample light to work properly, then the windows must be cleaned! You see!

GREENE Oh, I do now, sir. You make it very clear.

PENNY Naturally. And this . . .

Greene groans.

PENNY . . . 'To exterminate rats — one thousand pounds.' You see! A proper and necessary . . . RATS?

GREENE We had rather a lot of trouble with them, sir.

PENNY A lot of trouble?

GREENE There were rather a lot of them. You couldn't leave your hat about, sir.

PENNY Hat? Did you say 'hat' or 'rat'?

GREENE Er, both, sir. The . . . the rats used them — the hats, that is, as their nests. Any sort of hat — they loved them.

PENNY Oh! Really!

GREENE They ate the cheeses —

PENNY Of course they did. That's what rats do.

GREENE Fought the dogs and killed dozens of cats — we had a lot of complaints from old people —

PENNY They always complain. Never satisfied with what we do for them.

GREENE And several babies were bitten – in their cots – and the noise was terrible, all different squeaks and shrieks, you couldn't hear yourself think.

PENNY That's enough, that's enough. So . . . how did you get rid of them. (*Looking under the desk anxiously.*) They have gone, haven't they?

GREENE Yes, sir. Oh yes.

PENNY Did you use poison?

GREENE Well . . . no.

PENNY It was gas, then?

GREENE No . . . we . . . er (*a flash of inspiration*) called in an expert, sir.

PENNY (*impressed*) Ah! And what did he do?

GREENE (*awkwardly*) Well, this might be a bit difficult to understand, sir. He was very unusual – bit strange – and funny-coloured clothes . . . .

PENNY Oh . . . a student, was he? Looking for some easy money, no doubt, like the rest of them. Wouldn't surprise me if the sight of him didn't scare them away.

GREENE (*quickly*) No, sir – all he did was – play his bagpipes and all the rats followed him.

PENNY (*slowly, trying to grasp this*) The rats followed him?

GREENE Yes, they all came out of hiding and went off down the street. They seemed to like the music.

PENNY The rats followed an oddly dressed student playing the bagpipes. I see . . . Mr Greene, do you find this work rather a strain?

GREENE No, sir.

PENNY A little holiday, perhaps?

GREENE Holiday, sir? I've just had one, sir. I'm fine.

PENNY All right. Go on.

GREENE Then he led them to the river where they all . . . drowned.

PENNY (*after a pause*) Drowned. (*Long pause.*) A thousand pounds.

Arkwright, the Town Clerk, hiccupping from a rich dinner and a little too much brandy, blusters in like a small typhoon.

ARKWRIGHT Aye, Mr Penny, a thousand pounds! One thousand pounds is what that young scallywag wants from us. For a few drowned rats! It's a dam' sight too much — and there's nought to spare!

PENNY I must agree, Mr Arkwright, that such an expenditure hardly seems proper — and certainly isn't wise.

ARKWRIGHT Aye, as I said — can't pay, won't pay, and t'ain't worth it. (*Telephone rings.*) Mr Greene, answer that, lad.

GREENE Yes, sir. (*Listens, then offers 'phone to the Town Clerk.*) For you, sir. (*Hoarse whisper.*) It's *him*, sir. The Scot.

ARKWRIGHT (*on 'phone*) Arkwright, Town Clerk here. What do you want?

PIPER (*on 'phone*) Ha' ye got me money? Wha'? I done the wee job for you an' I wan' me pay an' noo nonsense.

ARKWRIGHT I tell thee, lad, once an' for all, you asked too much. You did dam' all an' you'll get nought. We spend our brass properly here.

PIPER I'm warning ye, Mr Town Clerk, I'll ha' me money if I have t'come and an' squeeze it out of your fat belly, you mean old skinflint. You'll no cheat me.

ARKWRIGHT Nay, lad, we'll have none o' that name-callin', you idle layabout. Get yoursel' a decent job, lad.

PIPER Ye'll soon see what a bonny worker I am. I'll play me pipes an' I'll call the tune — an' you'll nae like it when you see every lad and lassie following me. And ye'll see them nae more. (*Slams 'phone down.*)

ARKWRIGHT I told thee he were no good. Threatening *me*, Mr Arkwright, threatening the Town Clerk! Why, if he took all t'kids, it'd be the greatest kidnapping in the whole of history!

GREENE But Mr Arkwright, sir . . .

ARKWRIGHT Aye, what is it, lad?

GREENE Well, sir, if the rats followed him . . . the children might.

ARKWRIGHT Aye! You've followed me thinkin', lad. Get on that 'phone an' get me the police — an' the Education — an' the doctor an' —

PENNY A word in your ear, Mr Arkwright, if you please.

They move aside from Greene who pretends not to listen.

PENNY I think we might be able to turn this . . . er . . . situation to our mutual benefit, Mr Arkwright.

ARKWRIGHT Eh? What's that? Go on, Mr Penny, go on.

PENNY As well as for . . . er . . . the public good.

ARKWRIGHT Get t'point, Mr Penny.

PENNY The point is, Mr Arkwright, if all the children go, if they follow this wretched piper fellow, we could make a few valuable savings. You see?

ARKWRIGHT Aye! No.

PENNY No children — no schools. No education bills — no teachers to pay, no meals to provide, no paper to waste and no truant officers. Savings, Mr Arkwright, savings all round.

ARKWRIGHT Aye . . . just my thinkin', Mr Penny. Mr Greene — don't bother with those calls, now. I think I can hear a grand procession comin' up 'Igh Street, right now. Let's give 'em a wave as they go by.

Players and the play

Comedies make us laugh. Sometimes they're unlikely, or exaggerated and full of accidents and obvious misunderstandings, just to make us laugh. But some comedies make us think as well as laugh. Satire is a form of comedy that makes us laugh at people who are not normally funny. The characters in 'The expert' take themselves very seriously. The play makes us laugh at them and it makes us think whether they are really as important and sensible as they think they are.

Writing and discussion

- Make a selection of recent political cartoons. Discuss what is attacked and how it is done.
- Write a satire of your own. Be less kind to your characters than 'The expert' is.

15   Acceptance

Players	You – boy or girl Mother Father Friend
Place	The home of the boy or girl.
The refusal	This play contains the idea of the boy or girl refusing to go some-where. Exactly where and why is not stated in the play. This can be decided by the players after reading through 'The reason' below, and the play itself.
The reason	The boy or girl's refusal may be about returning to school after a long absence, perhaps due to illness – or truanting. It may concern a change of school or some fear about school such as being bullied or made fun of. There are other possibilities: going to Court or to the doctor or the hospital. Of course the refusal may have nothing to do with *where* the boy or girl must go. It could be something personal, perhaps connected with some worries about the family – money, clothes, family quarrels, the death of a relative.
The friend	Who the friend is must depend on what reasons you decide on for the refusal. Who would be most helpful? Who would be able to 'get through' to the boy or girl when the parents can't? So the friend could be a school friend or a relative of the family – uncle or aunt or grandparent. It may be an adult who knows the boy or girl well, such as a club leader or teacher. It may be one of the many people whose job is to help people: social worker, welfare officer, doctor or probation officer.
Action	There is nowhere to hide. So you march to the armchair and fix yourself into it like a suit of armour. Your body is as set as your white face. You will not go. Your father comes in, hard, looking for you. – All right, I'm tell-ing you, enough of these games, I've had enough, you've got to go, you're going to go, I'm taking you.

You speak one word: No. Now your father looks more puzzled than angry. He knows he can't just shout you into going. He sits down, making an effort at control. He speaks firmly, trying to understand, trying to be kind. But nothing gets through. You keep your head down.

He gets up, offering help. You are far away. He goes out shaking his head, feeling angry, feeling hurt. You wait, half-aware of a conversation outside the door. Then your mother comes in.

She's trying to look on the bright side: if you pretend there's nothing wrong it'll go away. She's restless about the room, sitting down close beside you, changing to another chair facing you, getting up, twitching at the curtains, touching her small ornaments on the shelf.

As she moves the chatter runs on smoothly, brightly. – Oh come on, dear, cheer up, it's all right, it'll be all right, don't be silly, nothing to fret about, is it, I know how you feel, but don't let it get you down, feeling better now, that's right, that's good, come on then off we go.

Somehow you've started to listen. You feel your shoulders ease down and your head comes up. Your eyes flicker, following your mother's small, swift movements towards the door. But the refusal is still in your mind and won't release your body.

The chatter stops as the door closes behind her. Then the half-heard sounds outside and the sudden odd silences. You wait – but now you feel . . . uncomfortable. You twist in the chair as new thoughts force into your mind. Shut them out, shut them out – they don't understand, they don't really care, why should I think about them?

Something's happening outside. There's new sounds, a new voice, a sort of greeting and muttered rapid words and some other strange sounds not quite words. But this time you're ready. You are not going to go.

Someone you know, a friend, comes in with that old smile, saying little, sitting down quietly beside you, knowing how you feel. When you start to talk, finding the words difficult, trying to explain, your friend nods and listens, watching your face.

As your head comes up and your eyes focus on your friend, you know that something has changed. What has happened? What is it that you feel? When your friend asks you to go you do not smile. But you say Yes quickly and get up. On the way out with your friend you feel like smiling.

Playlines
This family play can be seen in various ways by changing the casting for each of four performances:
First time: normal casting – mother, father, friend, boy or girl.
Second time: You (boy or girl) and your father change over roles.
Third time: You and your mother change over roles.
Fourth time: You and your friend change over roles.
Discuss this experience of seeing the boy or girl through the eyes of mother, father and friend.

- Group play: Show what happened before this refusal scene. What brought about this behaviour? What signs were there that something was wrong? Was the trouble talked about or ignored or simply not noticed?

  Several scenes might be necessary, some showing how the friend becomes involved in the situation.

Viewpoint
- Have you ever absolutely refused to do something? What happened?
- Describe how the father tries to deal with the situation as shown in the play.
- Why does the father go out 'feeling angry, feeling hurt'?
- Describe how the mother tries to deal with the situation. Compare her approach with that of her husband. Why does she appear to be more successful?
- How does the boy or girl react to what is said by each parent?
- Why is the friend able to succeed where the parents have failed?
- There are 'half-heard sounds outside and sudden odd silences' after the father leaves the room. What do you think is happening outside the door?
- When the friend arrives there are, among the other sounds of greeting and talking, 'some other strange sounds not quite words'. What do you think these strange sounds are?
- Why does the boy or girl 'feel like smiling' on the way out?

● Is 'Acceptance' a good title for this play? Can you suggest another?

Writing   ● Poem or story based on the theme of this play.

16 Paul

A series of family encounters

Players	Any number of pairs or groups of four players Paul Mother Father Friend of Paul, boy or girl
Play	This play deals with the most important and familiar relationships we have as members of a particular family. Paul's relationship with his parents is shown through a series of ten family situations or 'encounters'.
Casting	Each pair can work on its own for the first five encounters and then join another pair for the final five encounters. A group of four may prefer to work together all the time. In this case, each pair acts and watches in turn for encounters 1–5.
Place	As indicated in each encounter. A few chairs and a table are usually sufficient. A more detailed set could be prepared for any performance by all the groups.
Paul's family	Read through the situation below, talking it over as you go and when you have finished it. Paul finds it difficult to get on with his father. His father finds it equally difficult to get on with his son. There are no really open quarrels with blazing rows, but the house is full of tension. There is irritability, frustration, anger and, just as threatening, silence. Paul now challenges every word and move of his father. Even the simplest and most ordinary meeting — say, over the breakfast table or on the stairs — rapidly builds in tension and becomes painful to both. Paul's father reacts by trying to remain very calm when explaining how he feels about Paul's behaviour (both in and out of the house); he recognises, he thinks, Paul's growing need for independence, but is certain there must be proper signs of a sense of responsibility.

Paul's reaction is mainly to steer clear of his father whenever possible, and to defend his feelings and principles in the face of all his father's threats and opposition. He feels he is not trusted; his father treats him like a baby.

Paul's mother tries to remain neutral, but she does sometimes feel that her husband is hard on Paul, and that sometimes Paul is cheeky to his father. She is left feeling helpless and unhappy. Paul frequently forces an alliance with his mother against his father, saying that 'she understands even if you don't'. To Paul's father this looks as if Paul is taking over as 'the master' of the house, pushing him out.

Encounters 1–5

After your discussion, take a closer look at the family in action in encounters 1–5. These concentrate on Paul and his father, leaving out his mother. These two are placed in situations where they must encounter the thoughts and feelings of each other. They may react with silence or by walking away or with physical tension. But whatever they do, they will show the nature of their relationship.

Each encounter will normally last only a few minutes. As the work progresses and you become more involved in the situation, the playing time will extend quite naturally.

When you begin, keep in mind that you are a member of *this* particular family *living* the problems and relationships described in 'Paul's family'.

Encounters

1 Meeting on the stairs first thing in the morning.
2 Meeting in room with TV in the evening.
3 Giving: father's birthday.
4 Receiving: Paul's birthday.
5 Car journey to see car that father is thinking of buying.

Discussion

The performance and discussion of these five encounters will enable you to see and feel Paul's situation more clearly and personally.

Remember that other pairs will understand – and act – the relationships in each encounter in different ways, according to their own feelings and experience.

Role reversal

You can see these same five encounters from a different point of view using role reversal. This means that the two players change over roles: father plays Paul, and Paul plays his father.

You now see and feel the situation in a new way: *as* the other person. Replay the five encounters in these reversed roles.

Discuss afterwards.

Experiment
1 Reverse roles several times *during* any encounter at the suggestion of someone watching. Try this with an encounter of your choice.

2 This can be tried by groups of four players. Cast the mother in addition to the players already cast as Paul and his father. The mother can appear in any encounter of your choice at the same time as her husband and son, or before or after the encounter with her only son.

The fourth player in the group can observe and comment on the changes made by the mother's presence, or take turns playing the mother.

Encounters 6–10
The last five encounters place Paul in situations with both his parents. Sometimes both are present, sometimes he meets them separately, but both parents are involved in the situation.

Paul's parents may also meet when Paul is not there and discuss their *own* feelings as well as talking about their son. This concentrates the action on *their* relationship not only as parents but as husband and wife.

Casting
Pairs join up to form groups of four. Encounters, 6, 7, 8 and 9 require three players as mother, father and Paul. Encounter 10 also requires a friend of Paul's.

The fourth player, when not cast, acts as observer or takes turns playing the mother. The players of Paul and his father should not be changed.

Encounters
6 A *typical* family meal.
7 Help: father wants Paul to do a job.
8 Wanting: Paul needs some extra money.
9 Help: Paul's in trouble (at school/with the police . . .).
10 Visitor: Paul brings home a friend (boy or girl).

Discussion
After playing through, discuss your work. Does Paul get on with one parent better than the other? Why? How do Paul's parents get on with one another? When is Paul happy? What does he expect

61

from his parents? What do they expect from him? What makes them happy? How do you feel about them as a family?

Role reversal

Reverse the roles of father and son and replay these five encounters. Discuss afterwards.

Experiments

1 Reverse roles of father and Paul several times during any encounter of your choice at the suggestion of someone watching.

2 Replay any of these encounters *without* the mother so that they deal directly with the father–son relationship.

Discuss these experiments.

If people could see themselves and step into the thoughts and feelings of others, then some of the tension and conflict might be reduced and give a chance of building better relationships.

Complete your work by showing such an improvement in the whole family relationship, particularly between Paul and his father. It may be brought about through the efforts of a friend or relative or through a serious incident which makes everyone stop and think and try again. Show this change by replaying, after discussion, some of these encounters or some of your own.

17   Jane

A series of family encounters

Players
Any number of pairs or groups of four players
Jane
Julia
Mother
Father

Play
Like 'Paul' (page 57), this play deals with the most important and familiar relationships we have as members of a particular family. Jane's relationship with her parents and sister is shown through a series of ten family situations or 'encounters'.

Casting
Each pair can work on its own for the first five encounters and then join another pair for the final five encounters.

A group of four may prefer to work together all the time. In this case each pair acts and watches in turn for encounters 1–5.

Place
As indicated in each encounter. A few chairs and a table are usually sufficient. A more detailed set could be prepared for any performance by all the groups.

Jane's family
Read through the situation below, talking it over as you go and when you have finished it.

Jane feels lost and frightened in her own home. She has become increasingly nervous of other people, even ones she knows quite well – but she finds being with her mother the most difficult of all.

To an outsider, Jane's home seems warm and friendly until it is felt that Jane's relationship with her mother creates a cold and nervous tension.

Jane feels that both her parents, but especially her mother, prefer her younger sister Julia who, in her cheerful, chatty way, gets everything she wants and is liked by everyone. Jane feels ashamed of this feeling of jealousy and tries to make up for it by being very generous to Julia, always praising her and letting her have her own way.

Jane has withdrawn into a shell of little activity or speech which she feels will prevent her from further hurt — and from hurting others. She eats so little that her weight is sometimes a cause of concern, especially when the family are eating together.

She now finds every meeting with her family or other people painful and threatening. She reacts with her body tense, her hands raised as if to protect her, her arms wrapping her body as if to ward off blows. The tension reduces her voice to a whisper, and her eyes avoid others' as much as possible.

Julia seems unaware of the feelings she creates in Jane and simply thinks that she is 'ill' or 'odd' or 'being silly and difficult'. She does her best to 'help' her sister by encouragement, good advice and her 'Don't be silly' attitude.

Jane's mother is coolly distant: she appears as unaware of Jane's real feelings as Julia. Her daughter is a mystery to her, 'But she'll probably grow out of it'. Why one daughter should be so happy and bright and normal and the other so different is something she either can't or won't consider deeply. Her chief reaction to Jane's behaviour is not to see it — simply ignore it and it will go away.

Jane's father is mainly notable by his absence on business. He behaves as if everyone, even his wife, were strangers to him, though Julia always welcomes him with her typical enthusiasm. His sudden appearances at home seem God-like, commanding respect rather than love — an arrangement which seems perfectly satisfactory to him.

Jane likes drawing animals, playing the guitar and riding. The family owns the horse which she shares with Julia. All these interests allow her to do what she most wants to do — to be by herself.

Encounters 1–5

After your discussion, take a closer look at the family in action in encounters 1–5. These concentrate on Jane and her mother, leaving out her sister and father. These two are placed in situations where they must encounter the thoughts and feelings of each other. They may react with silence or by walking away or with physical tension. But whatever they do, they will show the nature of their relationship.

Each encounter will normally last only a few minutes. As the work progresses and you become more involved in the situation, the playing time will extend quite naturally.

When you begin, keep in mind that you are a member of *this* particular family *living* the problems and relationships described in 'Jane's family'.

Encounters
1 Meeting in the kitchen on a busy morning.
2 Giving: mother's birthday.
3 Meeting in Jane's room in the evening.
4 Help: mother wants to plan a birthday surprise for Julia.
5 Car journey together to collect father at station.

Discussion
The performance and discussion of these five encounters will enable you to see and feel Jane's situation more clearly and personally.

Remember that other pairs will understand – and act – the relationships in each encounter in different ways, according to their own feelings and experience.

Role reversal
You can see these same five encounters from a different point of view using role reversal. This means that the two players change over roles: mother plays Jane, and Jane plays her mother.

You now see and feel the situation in a new way: *as* the other person. Replay the five encounters in these reversed roles.

Discuss afterwards.

Experiments
1 Reverse roles several times *during* any encounter at the suggestion of someone watching. Try this with an encounter of your choice.
2 This can be tried by groups of four players. Cast Jane's sister Julia in addition to the players already cast as Jane and her mother. Julia can appear in any encounter of your choice at the same time as her mother and sister, or before or after the encounter with only her sister.

The fourth player in the group can observe and comment on the changes made by the sister's presence, or take turns playing the sister (Julia).

Encounters 6–10
The last five encounters place Jane in situations with her mother and her sister, and sometimes her father as well. They are not

65

necessarily all present all the time: Jane may talk with her sister or to her father with the others absent.

The parents may also meet when neither of their children is present. They may discuss their own feelings as well as talking about Jane and Julia. This concentrates the action on *their* relationship not only as parents but as husband and wife.

Casting Pairs join up to form groups of four. Encounters 6, 7, 8 and 9 require three players as mother, Jane and Julia. Encounter 10 also requires a player as father.

The fourth player, when not cast, acts as observer or takes turns playing Julia. The players of Jane and her mother should not be changed.

Encounters 6 A *typical* family meal.
7 Receiving: mother and Julia help Jane to buy a dress.
8 Help: mother and Julia want Jane to help prepare the house for a party.
9 Wanting: Jane wants to compete in the local gymkhana – and so does Julia.
10 Greeting: father comes home unexpectedly for the weekend.

Discussion After playing through, discuss your work. When is Jane happy? What makes the other members of the family happy? What upsets each of them? Does Jane get on better with her mother when Julia is not there? Does the father's absence have any particular effect on the family?

Role reversal 1 Reverse the roles of Jane and Julia and replay any encounters of your choice.
2 Reverse the roles of Jane and her mother and replay encounters of your choice.

Discuss afterwards.

Experiments 1 Reverse the roles of Jane and Julia or Jane and her mother several times during any encounter of your choice at the suggestion of someone watching.
2 Replay any of these encounters without Julia so that they deal directly with the mother – eldest daughter relationship.
3 Replay any of these encounters with all the family present – mother, Jane, Julia – and father.

Discuss this second part of your work.

Complete your work by showing such an improvement in the whole family relationship, particularly between Jane and her mother. It might be brought about through the efforts of a friend or relative, or through a serious incident which makes everyone stop and think and try again. Show this change by replaying, after discussion, some of these encounters or some of your own.

Players and the play

We all have problems and difficulties of some kind, perhaps not very much though they seem big at the time. Because you can cope and not get hurt too much you think that it's the same for everyone else. Just trying to understand one person like Paul or Jane makes you more aware and sympathetic. When you act their family situation, you enter their experience of how it feels, how a word or a look can make all the difference between feeling good and feeling bad. Sometimes your own feelings are touched — there is a connection between something in the encounter and your own life. You explore yourself in a safe and private way. Watching the encounters is a way of learning how families behave, but playing different roles in the family means that you see every character from the inside and the outside.

Writing and discussion

- Describe how you responded personally to either Jane or Paul — as individuals.
- Has playing family roles — and role reversal — helped you in any way to understand the feelings of other people?
- Do you think there is a danger that playing encounters like these will only cause (or increase) embarrassment, anxiety and even ridicule? Does this matter?
- What differences did you find between watching an encounter and acting an encounter? Which did you prefer doing?
- Describe a play (at school, in a theatre or on TV) that dealt with family life in a way that seemed honest and true to you. Did you identify with one particular character?

18   Love is all

A play in eight scenes

Players
: Barb
Ginger – her friend
Barb's mum
Barb's dad
Office worker on the bus
Record shop assistant

Numbers
: If the play is improvised after reading the script, other parts can be added for boys or girls in the bus, record shop and coffee bar scenes.

    The scenes can be cast and rehearsed separately and then brought together for performances.

Action
: *Scene one: Barb's home.*

MUM You in tonight?

BARB Dunno. Might do my hair. (*Switches on TV.*) When's tea?

MUM Mrs Whatsit, you know, Barb, she was telling me about that friend of yours, what's her name, Ginger.

DAD She's no good.

BARB What's for tea then?

MUM She told me all about that disco you went to. That night you shouted up to the window.

DAD Out all hours.

MUM Said she'd get into trouble – if she wasn't already.

BARB We haven't got sausages again, have we? Oh.

MUM Said she should be taken into care, having no father and all that. I didn't know he was dead.

BARB He's in the nick.

DAD She'll go the same way.

BARB She's all right. It's not her fault. She's a good mate.

DAD She's no good.

BARB She's all right (*'Phone rings.*) That's for me. (*Runs to hall.*)

MUM If it's that girl, tell her you're not going out.

DAD She's no good.

Scene two: Telephone in the hall.

BARB Oh, hi, Ginge. You OK?

GINGER Yeh.

BARB What do you want? You going out?

GINGER Yeh.

BARB Who with? You going with Billy and the others?

GINGER Yeh.

BARB See you down the club, then?

GINGER Yeh.

BARB Eight all right?

GINGER Yeh. Hey, Barb, listen . . . (*she starts to giggle*) you know Mick, don't you . . . (*more giggles*)

BARB With the motor bike . . . (*she giggles*) and he's always shouting (*she starts to laugh*)

GINGER (*laughing*) He always shouts . . . and keeps on revving and revving and there's all this exhaust going — and he's — (*she can hardly speak for laughing*) disappearing in it and shouting all the time . . .

BARB He's mad!

GINGER He's crazy! Well he was sitting there, shouting, and he told me about Cathy . . .

BARB (*trying not to laugh*) Cathy, yeah, what did he say?

GINGER (*near hysterics*) So he said to her . . .

Both girls break down in screams of laughter.

Scene three: Next morning

MUM Did you have a nice time, Barb?

BARB Yeh. It was all right.

MUM Want another sausage?

BARB No.

MUM Where did you go?

BARB Just went around.

MUM With your friends?

BARB Yeh. Can you get me a coat, Mum?

DAD You've got a coat.

MUM Have you seen one then?

BARB Yeh — black leather — and it comes in like this — (*she shows her*)

DAD That grey one's practically new.

BARB Yeh – like the Ark.

DAD Plenty of good wear yet.

BARB Dad, I've had it ages – it's old fashioned. I look like some old grannie in it.

MUM You know what they cost . . .

BARB I'd put my money towards it.

DAD That's gone as fast as you get it. And then you want more.

MUM I'll have a look in the catalogue – see what we can manage. (*Door bell rings*.) I'll talk to your dad later. (*Rings again*.)

BARB That's Ginger.

DAD What's she want?

BARB Nothing. We're going down town, that's all. (*Puts on coat*.) Look at it. See what I mean? I feel like a freak. (*Bell rings again*.) All right. See you later.

DAD Don't get into trouble.

BARB (*as she goes*) Fat chance.

Scene four: On the bus, upstairs. The girls are laughing together.

BARB No, shut up, Ginge – did you have a good time?

GINGER What do you think? (*She laughs*.) How did you get on with Nicky?

BARB Oh he's all right, isn't he?

GINGER He's got some good gear.

BARB Yeh. See those shoes. And I had this horrible thing on.

(*Looks at her coat, and then at Ginger's black leather jacket*.)

GINGER Didn't say anything, did he?

BARB Oh no, he's not like that – but it's how you feel, isn't it?

GINGER Hey, we'll go down Bonny's, see if they've got any new stuff in. I got a great black top there.

BARB Did you? How much was it?

GINGER Nothing – if you're quick! (*She laughs loudly*.)

BARB You didn't! You knocked it off!

GINGER Sshh! Don't tell the world, they'll all want one!

BARB Oh shut up, Ginge, it's serious. You'll get caught.

GINGER Yeh, like me old man.

BARB What?

GINGER Nothing. Want a fag?

BARB Ta.

Ginger's matches are damp and won't strike.

GINGER I can't get a light, they're damp. You got any?

BARB Ask him. Go on.

GINGER Excuse me. I said, excuse me. Have you got a light?

OFFICE WORKER Pardon?

GINGER A light?

OFFICE WORKER Pardon?

GINGER Have you got a light? For . . . my . . . cig-ar-ette. (*She starts to laugh.*)

BARB Stop laughing, Ginge!

OFFICE WORKER How old are you?

BARB She's seventeen.

OFFICE WORKER Pardon?

GINGER And I got two kids.

BARB But her old man won't let her smoke indoors.

The man gets up, rings the bell.

GINGER Well, I like that!

BARB So do I.

GINGER (*very loudly*) Pardon? (*They both laugh.*)

OFFICE WORKER (*angrily*) You ought to be in Borstal! (*He goes downstairs.*)

GINGER If I went there I bet he'd be the Governor! (*Looking down out of the window.*) There he goes. He's looking up!

BARB Give him a wave. Wave, wave. (*They wave and laugh.*)

GINGER (*imitating*) 'You ought to be in Borstal'!

BARB (*laughing*) Pardon?

GINGER (*getting up*) Come on, Barb – and stop taking the mickey!

They run downstairs.

Scene five: Record shop. They are looking in the window.

GINGER So I said 'I'm never going out with you again'.

BARB Aren't you, Ginge?

GINGER No I'm not – unless he asks me!

BARB What if he doesn't?

GINGER See if I care. Want one? (*She offers sweets.*)

BARB Yes, like little pills, aren't they?

GINGER That's why I got 'em. I'll take a couple of orange, and four red and six blues. Get really high! Wowee!

BARB My mum's got some orange ones. She won't say what for.

GINGER I reckon my old girl's got the lot — except for one and she don't need that with me dad away.

BARB Shut up, Ginge, let's go in.

GINGER (*as they go in*) Ask him if he's got any records!

BARB Don't be daft. Get *Moonlight City*.

GINGER Yeh, it's not bad. I like *Love is all*. Get that.

They go into the listening booth and hear the record several times.

GINGER Great.

BARB Yeh.

GINGER How much you got?

BARB Not much. (*They check their money.*) And we need the fare back.

GINGER If I hadn't got those sweets and fags . . .

BARB I told you I didn't have much.

GINGER Where'd it all go?

BARB I told you. I'm saving up for a coat.

GINGER Yeh, you told me. And I told you I want that record.

BARB We'll come this afternoon.

GINGER I can't.

BARB Why not?

GINGER Nosey.

BARB All right.

GINGER 'Cause I'm baby-sitting, that's why.

BARB Oh. In the afternoon?

GINGER Yeh, in the afternoon, Me uncle — he's not really me uncle — he's taking me mum out shopping and stuff. He's got a car and a little kid called Shirley. And his wife's left him. Anything else you want to know?

BARB No, I mean I was only asking.

GINGER Forget it.

BARB We'd better go then.

GINGER You get the record.

BARB What?

GINGER It's on the rack. Just stick it under your coat.

BARB I can't.

GINGER Go on. I'll chat the bloke up. Go on. I can't get it under my coat, can I?

BARB I dunno.

GINGER It's dead easy with two of us. OK, Barb?

She goes to the counter. Barb goes to the records.

GINGER Excuse me. I've found some pills.

SHOP ASSISTANT Some pills?

GINGER Yeh, pills. Different colours. Look. (*She shows some.*)

SHOP ASSISTANT Did you find a bottle or anything?

GINGER Oh no. They're loose. All around on the floor – over there.

Barb takes the record and walks out.

GINGER I'll catch you up, Sandra. Look, I've got to be going.

SHOP ASSISTANT They might be dangerous. I'll see if I can find any more. Thanks anyway.

GINGER Sure. 'Bye. (*She goes out.*)

Scene six: Coffee bar. They are sitting at a small table.

BARB What you make me do it for?

GINGER I didn't make you.

BARB You did.

GINGER Pinchin's easy.

BARB Oh yeah. That's why I'm still shaking.

GINGER Didn't get caught, did you? And you know why?

BARB No – 'cause the bloke was blind?

GINGER No – 'cause I did the hard part.

BARB Oh yeah.

GINGER Who kept him busy then? Who made sure he wouldn't see you? Well then.

BARB Well, all right. I feel better now. I went like jelly though.

GINGER So did I.

BARB You didn't.

GINGER My voice kept going funny like. I was sure he'd notice. I couldn't get out of there fast enough.

BARB I'm not doing it again anyway. First time, last time.

GINGER As long as you don't get caught — that's what me dad says.

BARB He would. You know what my dad says? Don't get into trouble.

GINGER Well, you haven't.

BARB He'd call this trouble all right. He'd kill me.

GINGER He probably couldn't care less.

BARB Yours wouldn't!

GINGER That's where you're wrong, Miss Clever!

BARB Oh am I?

GINGER He's good to me. He gave me this leather jacket.

BARB Yeh. Yeh, he would. That's why he's —

GINGER Oh no it isn't! He bought this, bought it for me, I saw him! He gives me anything I want.

BARB After he's taken it from someone else.

She picks up the record and goes to the door.

GINGER Where are you going?

Barb goes out. Ginger gets up and follows her.

Scene seven: Record shop.
Barb goes in with the record hidden. She stands beside the rack. The shop assistant watches her. Ginger comes in.

SHOP ASSISTANT Get out!

GINGER What?

SHOP ASSISTANT You've had your joke. So clear off.

GINGER What are you talking about? What joke?

SHOP ASSISTANT I don't want your sort in here.

GINGER What makes you so fussy?

SHOP ASSISTANT Are you going? (*He comes round the counter towards her.*)

Barb puts the record back.

SHOP ASSISTANT Get out, you little tart.

GINGER I'm going.

As she goes she blows him a kiss. Barb follows her out.

Scene eight: On the bus home.
Ginger is doing her nails. Barb is looking out of the window.

GINGER You all right, Barb?

BARB Yes.

GINGER You've gone all quiet.

BARB I'm thinking.

GINGER Sounds painful! (*She laughs and Barb grins.*)

BARB You're a good mate.

GINGER Yeah, that's what they all say.

BARB Thanks, anyway.

GINGER What for?

BARB For playing him up.

GINGER Forget it.

BARB I was stuck there, with him looking at me. I couldn't have done it without you.

GINGER Yeh, well, it was my fault in the first place.

BARB What?

GINGER I got you into it. Only fair. Anyway, I told me dad . . .

BARB What? Go on, Ginge.

GINGER Well, when I see him – Visiting Days, you know – he always says, Keep out of trouble and I say, Yeah, I'll be good . . . and he'd do anything for me, I know he would.

BARB Well, we didn't take the record, did we?

GINGER (*starting to laugh*) No, we just borrowed it for a bit.

BARB They can't say we've worn it out! (*They both laugh.*)

GINGER (*loudly*) Hardly used!

BARB (*louder*) Pardon!

GINGER (*imitating*) Get out you little tart!

BARB You ought to be in Borstal!

GINGER Pardon!

19   Points of conflict

This is a series of play situations divided into two Programmes. Programme 1 forms a complete unit. It should be played first. Programme 2 develops the material in the first programme. The activities in Programme 2 may be selected in any order.

Programme 1

Players

Groups of four or more
Mother — one player
Father — one player
Son — played in turn by each boy
Daughter — played in turn by each girl

Play

This play looks at one typical conflict between parents and son or daughter. In a series of four 'explorations' the conflict moves from the parents' asking to their demanding, and from the child's agreeing to his or her direct refusal.

In these explorations there is only *one* child — a son *or* a daughter. Each player cast as son or daughter is really playing the same child — but with their own individual reactions. A player may refer to brothers or sisters if he and she wishes, but they do not appear in the situation.

Place

Usually a room for which a few chairs, TV (another chair) and table are sufficient. A more detailed set showing the family living room and your 'untidy' room could be prepared for any performance by all the groups.

Starting

Read through the following 'Conflict situation'.
Discuss the two lists of attitudes.
Cast and work through explorations 1–4.

Conflict situation

There are many familiar conflicts which can arise between you and your parents — even if you happen to get on well with one another most of the time. The conflict may be over money: how much *you* want, how much they are prepared to give. It may arise over the friends you go with, the time you come home at night or just how much you help about the house. Sometimes the issue gets more personal – your girlfriend or boyfriend, your clothes, hair-style, general attitude to things . . . almost anything. The conflict lies in how the particular issue is dealt with by each 'side'. How much do you insist on what you want to do – how reasonable or firm or angry are your parents? Can you have a fair and reasonable discussion about it or does it have to become a shouting match? Can you change people's attitudes – or reach some sort of compromise?

The starting point of this conflict is: as a parent you want your son or daughter to clear up his or her room. The issue is as simple and ordinary as that. At the moment when the first 'exploration' starts there is no conflict: simply something someone wants done.

Attitudes Read through and discuss the following lists of attitudes which might be aroused by this issue.

As a parent, mother or father, you want the job done because:
1 Although your room is usually all right, it really is a mess at the moment.
2 The room's not too bad, but it's getting worse all the time.
3 You feel like a thorough 'spring clean' – and that means *all* the rooms.
4 You feel your son/daughter needs a good 'shake-up'.
5 You don't mind what it's like usually, but visitors are coming.
6 You are getting sick and tired of asking for it to be done.
7 You feel your son/daughter is old enough to take care of things properly instead of having everything done for him/her.
8 That room is always in a terrible mess.
9 You feel your son/daughter treats your home like a hotel and does nothing to help.
10 You thing it's time you put your foot down about certain things and this will do for a start.

As the son or daughter you don't want to do this job because:
1 You can't be bothered.
2 It's not your job.
3 You're too busy.
4 You're too tired.
5 It's all right, anyway.
6 It's *your* room, isn't it?
7 You don't care what anybody else thinks of it.

8 You like it as it is.

9 You don't like being *told* what to do.

10 No one else tidies up.

Explorations The parents are played throughout Programme 1 as friendly, reasonable parents whose son or daughter usually co-operates without any trouble.

Try to keep the same players as parents for all four explorations. The son or daughter can be played as each player wishes, following the guidelines given in each exploration.

Playing time Some of these meetings between parent and child in the first exploration will be very brief, lasting a minute or so. In some very little may be said though a facial expression or a movement may say a lot. There may be long silences or a direct question and answer. Each 'child' can react in his or her own way.

Explorations 1 *Asking and agreeing*

After casting parents and other players as son or daughter, decide which 'child' will play first, second and so on. In a mixed group alternate boy and girl.

The mother plays the exploration with the first son or daughter. The father watches with the other players. The two players decide how to begin – they may be in the same room or different rooms; they may be busy or working or watching TV, whatever they like.

During this scene the mother asks the son or daughter to clear up his or her room. Keep in mind that the mother is being played as a friendly, reasonable parent who usually gets full co-operation.

The son or daughter can react to this asking in slightly different ways, ending by agreeing to do the job. You, as the son or daughter, may show:

1 cheerful agreement, even willingness;

2 straightforward agreement – OK, then, I'll do it;

3 a willing-to-please agreement;

4 a reluctant agreement;

5 a very reluctant agreement;

and similar ideas of your own.

The scene should be quickly ended after the son or daughter has agreed to do the job.

Now the second player plays the situation as son or daughter with mother. Continue until all the players have played the situation.

Mother is now replaced by father. The situation is replayed with the father asking for the job to be done. Each player plays son or daughter as before.

The mother watches the action: she can see how each 'child' reacts to the other parent. The players themselves will notice differences in their playing to each parent.

Complete this first exploration by discussing how parents and children talk to one another, particularly when it involves getting something done. Discuss the differences you noticed as a 'parent' or as a 'child'.

Then follow the same working methods for Exploration 2.

2 *A kind of refusal*
Play the parents the same way as before, but now the acceptances from the son or daughter become various forms of refusal. You don't actually say you won't do it – only not yet – in your own good time. You may indicate that:
1 you meant to do it, of course you did, but you 'forgot';
2 you'll clear it up later – not now;
3 you're tired – you'll do it tomorrow;
4 you've got nowhere to put anything – but you'll try to find somewhere – later;
5 you're too busy – homework, going out;
and ideas of your own.

Repeat these refusals with father asking.

Discuss any differences of feeling you notice between the playing of these refusals and the acceptances made in Exploration 1. Comment on how each parent deals with the various refusals.

3 *Definite refusals*
Still play the same kind of parent who now receives a more definite refusal. Parent and child are beginning to reach a point of conflict. You may indicate that:
1 you can't be bothered;

2 it's not your job;

3 it's all right anyway;

4 it's *your* room.

Repeat these definite refusals with father asking. Don't let these 'refusals' become bitter quarrels. The parents can:

1 try a bit of gentle bribery;

2 let the matter drop for now;

3 ignore the refusal and *expect* the job to be done;

4 make a vague threat about something – and leave the matter to your good sense.

Discuss the results of these explorations.

The real point of conflict is reached in Exploration 4.

4 *Demand and refusal*

Now both sides, parents and son or daughter are caught up in a conflict of strong feelings. The demand is as strong as the refusal and neither wants to give way to the other.

Play mother and father as now being sick and tired of having to ask you to tidy up your room: it's always a mess – and they want something done about it *now*. The asking has become a demand. In your refusal, you may indicate that:

1 You *do* clear it up, but there's nowhere to put anything, the room's too small, you have to do everything there, you haven't got time to make it look like a showroom, who sees it anyway?

2 Why should you have to do all the work in the house, you've got a lot to do, it's all right anyway, don't keep on about it, it's your room, isn't it?

3 Why are people always going on about it being clean and tidy, it looks OK to you, no one else sees it, it's your room you can do what you like there, can't you, your friends can do what they like with their rooms, no one keeps on at them.

4 It's not a mess, it's the way you like to organise things, *you* know where everything is, they're your things, your records, your clothes, you take care of stuff, it's OK.

5 What mess? There's no mess, that's how all your mates' rooms look, it's great, you can relax there, could do with a portable TV, thinking of spraying the windows green, you don't mind if

someone gives it a bit of a broom over so long as they don't touch anything, what is there to worry about?

Repeat these forms of refusal with father asking.

The group leader should end these situations after a given time, but some might end with the parent walking off to let the situation cool down.

Discussion   Complete your work on Programme 1 by discussing how a simple, ordinary issue can become a conflict which creates bad feelings between parent and child.

Does one conflict create others, so that there are bad feelings over a number of small issues? Players can discuss their own experiences of difficulties arising over similar small issues. Some of these could be used for your own 'Points of conflict' explorations.

Discuss how these conflicts can be settled. Players can describe how they settle or try to settle theirs.

You can continue this work – with new aspects of conflict and attempts to find solutions – in Programme Two. The same 'conflict situation' material is the basis of this programme as well. The explorations can be selected in any order.

Programme 2

Explorations 5 *Conflict with both parents*
Place both parents opposite the son or daughter. Both come forward into the asking-situation. One parent may feel more strongly or less strongly than the other about the issue, but they are *united in their disapproval* of your room and in wanting something done. One parent may say little or nothing, but *both* are present – and the son or daughter will have to react to both and refuse both.

For this work, repeat some of the previous Explorations – for example, Explorations 2 and 4.

Discuss the differences you observe when both parents are present compared with the occasions when only one parent did the asking.

6 *Parents in conflict with one another*
Again, both parents are present in the situation. Now they themselves are in conflict over this issue. The thoughts and feelings

which divide them can be shown *before* the son or daughter is asked to clear up the room. They may try to present a united front, but their real, individual feelings gradually emerge.

Select some of the previous Explorations (such as 3 and 4) for this work or try some ideas of your own.

Discuss the effect of the parents' conflict – which can range from mild disagreement to totally opposed attitudes – on the situation involving the son or daughter. You will also be able to observe how their reactions to the refusal differ.

7 *Friendly advice*
When we've got a problem – whether as parents or children – we turn to our friends. They may only listen, and that can help; they may sympathise or offer advice; and sometimes they can tell us that *we* are the ones who are 'in the wrong'. We try to see the situation through the eyes of people who are not involved – a more objective viewpoint.

First, cast one player as the son or daughter; the other players are your friends. You can talk to them one at a time or a couple of friends may call to see you. You might meet all of them at a club or cafe.

You can tell them your troubles: the situation might be getting angry and unpleasant as in Exploration 4 where there's been demands and refusals; or it might still be in the irritating stage as in Exploration 2 and 3.

After your attempt as the son or daughter, the rest of the group can try this role in turn. End by discussing how each player deals with the situation and what help he or she obtains.

Then cast one player as the mother or the father; the other players as the parent's friends. As the parent, you meet your friends and talk about your present difficulties with your son or daughter.

The other players try the role of parent in turn. You can try it with the mother and father *both* meeting the friends. End the work with a discussion.

8 *Experiencing the role of parent and child*

When, for example, father and son are arguing, it would help each to understand something of the other's point of view if they could step into one another's shoes – 'become' the other person. This can be done by role reversal.

While father and son *or* mother and daughter are playing a situation, they are asked to reverse roles from time to time. The father now plays as the son, and the son plays as the father. They can continue the situation in their new roles or *replay* all or part of the previous work. The two instructions, (1) to reverse roles and (2) to continue or replay, should be given by one of the watching group.

Role reversal may be suggested at any point, but particularly interesting points will arise – a certain attitude, a repeated reaction, words or special movements of the body. These can be explored by both players (and the watching group) through a 'reversal' at that moment. The son or daughter will see what the situation is like as a parent, and the parent as a child.

Choose any of the previous Explorations for this work, discussing the experience of role reversal with the actual players.

9 *Changing the playing of the parents*

Players have been instructed to play the parents in the same way throughout as friendly, reasonable people with no particular difficulties between themselves or with their children. Now all the previous Explorations can be re-examined by changing the playing of the parents. The group may decide to present different parents for each Exploration – some arising from discussion, others directly from experience; or to present one set of new parents throughout the series of Explorations.

10 *A group 'Exploration' play*

The work you have done so far may be drawn together in discussion for the preparation of a complete group play based on this, or a similar, family issue. This is a 'play' in the sense that it is prepared, rehearsed and presented as a complete statement. It may still use many of the Exploration techniques so that several aspects of the situation may be shown and the basic attitudes and feelings revealed. You can use a form of television treatment by having a 'voice over' narrator to link the 'cutting' from one 'shot' or scene to another.

Players and the play
Most of our group plays begin with deciding on a story-line or plot – what is going to happen. But sometimes we begin with a character (like a corrupt businessman), or a social issue (like nuclear power), or a feeling (like frustration or jealousy) or a situation (like an argument). When we do this, we don't need a lot of action or a lot of different scenes or things happening all the time. We have one situation, one group of people and one place. Then we explore what is in each character's head in that situation. That is where the vital action is, and if we work hard at it, the plays are just as exciting and sometimes more interesting than action drama.

Writing and discussion
- Do you enjoy TV programmes with a lot of action in them? Do you act this kind of play yourself?
- What do your play discussions usually begin with – story, character, idea, feeling, viewpoint?
- Do you feel that the vital action is in our heads? How can you show that in a play?

20   Home

<table>
<tr><td>Players</td><td>From seven to whole class
Group of squatters — at least three
Group of police — at least two
Group of demolition workers — at least two
Reporters — newspapers and TV — at least one
Officials from the Town Hall — at least one</td></tr>
<tr><td>Place</td><td>A derelict house in a Victorian terrace due for demolition. The action takes place inside and outside the house.</td></tr>
<tr><td>Numbers</td><td>For a group of seven, cast the minimum in each group as above and have the demolition workers double-up as the reporter and the Town Hall official.

Increase each group according to numbers available.

Other players can be cast as neighbours (from the 'safe' houses across the street — though they may be afraid that it will be their turn next for demolition) and as passers-by. These can express individual as well as group reactions.</td></tr>
<tr><td>Play</td><td>The play as set down here only indicates the viewpoint of each group. It should be regarded as a guide rather than a script to be followed exactly. Your first rehearsals and discussions about this kind of conflict should enable you to express clearer, more definite attitudes.

Some players may see the issues raised in this play quite differently from those indicated. They are free to change it to express their own attitudes and viewpoints.</td></tr>
<tr><td>**Action**</td><td>This is our house, our home: come on in. Break down that boarded-up window and climb in.

We clear up the mess, throw out the rubbish, clean out the toilet, discover the water's OK and the loo flushes, no gas, no light, but there's a good fireplace in the front room and a back-boiler stove in the kitchen and it's great.

Some of us bring in mattresses and blankets; some fix windows and doors and the dangerous stairway; others scrub out the kitchen — the sink's disgusting and the outlet has to be poked free.</td></tr>
</table>

And now there's food cooking and it's warm and there's a guitar playing and someone reading and others planning jobs for tomorrow and we're home, all of us, together.

Then, early in the morning, you come, crashing at our front door, shouting.

This is the police, open this door. You have illegal occupation of private property. You are requested to leave immediately. There is a demolition order on this property. Please leave now. Of course we know you'll be stubborn, you lot always are. All right so you're homeless, but we have to protect the rights of property owners whether we like it or not. It's our duty, understand?

As police, personal feelings don't enter into it. We just want you out, that's all. OK, so you're broke and you can't afford anywhere, well, that's not our problem. Try working for a change. We've got our job to do. So, out! Before we smash this door down.

From the upstairs window, with a collection of odd weapons and strange missiles, we watch and shout back, feeling anxious, being determined. We knew what it'd be like: it's happened before.

And you, the Press, arrive eager for action pictures and personal interviews, smelling the conflict of easy headlines.

As far as we reporters are concerned it's pretty routine, but something might develop. Check with the Town Hall about this demolition order. Get an interview with the ring-leader; and the police Inspector. Talk to the neighbours, local point of view, vandalism, noisy parties, drugs, all the usual lines. Get a shot when the police break in and maybe one of the group as they come out, especially if there's a bit of resistance.

We tell *our* story, but you've got it written already. The Inspector speaks seriously and humanely and you write down his dutiful words. As he speaks, the door gives way and there's police in the front and in the back and up the stairs and we're out in the street with our possessions chucked in a heap on the roadside.

Up the street we see you, the demolition team, already crumbling the end of the terrace, eating your way towards our shabby, warm house.

Well, mate, it's a job isn't it, got to be done, see. Load of rubbish this lot, rotting for years. It's fair work and good pay and there's a few bits of scrap on the side, like. Yer, we know there's no new houses, prices like bloomin' Everest for just an old room, see what I mean, and hard luck on anyone with nowhere, but it's a job, like I said.

We're left standing in the road feeling sore and pretty sick. Then we see this official give a paper to the Inspector. Can't believe it, still can't. A court order to stop the demolition! Someone wants to save these historic buildings — and half of them knocked down already! Brilliant!

We're back inside our old home before the police can pull out their whistles.

21   Cheap

Players	From nine to a whole class Lorry driver His mate, a young lad Officer Corporal Soldiers — at least one Terrorists — at least two Shoppers — at least two Lorry driver's wife and two children
Numbers	The play can be performed with the minimum numbers shown above. Some players could play two parts, including that of the wife and children. Larger numbers will give the play more substance and add vitality to the action as well as stimulating a greater range of reactions and attitudes.
Place	A country road; a lorry; an upstairs room overlooking the High Street; the High Street itself; Army barracks and the lorry driver's home are indicated in the script. Groups may bring in direct references to particular places and situations as they wish.
Play	Particular viewpoints, such as those of the soldiers and terrorists, are only indicated in the play as a guide to the group. Your first rehearsals and discussions about this kind of conflict should enable you to express clearer, more definite attitudes.
Action	We stop the lorry. It is a chilly damp early morning on the edge of town and there's better places to be. The driver, middle-aged, is terrified. By God! he's thinking, it's happening to me. He knows what we want.

His mate, a young lad, looks round him in a kind of wonder, almost enjoyment. To him it's some great adventure to talk about. He stares eagerly at our rifles and automatics. The man and the lad stand awkwardly in the road, the man shuffling and gasping, the lad half-grinning. A rifle barrel jabs into the man's fat beer-gut.

We know about his wife and two kids. We know where they live. He understands our meaning all right. He watches us fix the bomb just in front of the rear axle. Even the grinning lad understands now; and his smile freezes. We give the driver his instructions: the time, the place, his silence. He is sweating hard when he drives off.

It's all chatter and gossip on the country bus into town for the shopping. It's a lovely day now isn't it; bit misty at first though, really fine after so much rain but so cold when you get up. And before you know it we're turning into the car park by the High Street and getting our bags and baskets and coats and helping one another off, still talking and calling to those behind to hurry up.

Stand at — ease! Stand easy! You men: routine patrol duties. High Street, rear sector and return route as shown on this map. Which you have studied. Working method as per usual. Patrol both sides. Got that? Work in pairs, one forward of the other. All arms one round up and on 'safety'. All weapons will be cleaned and examined on return to base. Understood? Report anything suspicious immediately. Avoid individual actions. Do not retaliate to provocative action unless fire-arms are involved. Corporal!

Heard it all before, me and my platoon mates, hear it in our sleep. We get our tea and cheese wads and try to manage a quick drag at the same time. The officer and our corp. study the map — wouldn't know if it was upside down. We do a good job that's got to be done and we keep our heads down and look after our mates. But we look after No 1 first.

Outside the supermarket a lorry stops. The driver and his lad drop down from the cab. They look around anxiously, but their eyes constantly return to a black bulge near the rear axle. The lad points to a telephone box; the man coughs and shrugs. They walk towards the box and hesitate, the lad watching the driver. A quick call — police or military — that's all that's necessary. The lad pulls at the door. The driver hurries on.

Oh come on, dear, it's only round the corner; poor old dear, leg playing up something awful, don't worry, we're all getting on, aren't we? And there's the supermarket where the food's cheap and really good quality, a lovely piece of beef last week, and bargain offers as well; if she says another word about her daughter's wonderful wedding I'll strangle her.

The lad shouts at the driver's back. He runs forward a little and shouts again. Then, head down, he hurries to catch up.

So it's fags out and flags out and off to glory, boys! We take it pretty easy till we reach the lower end of the High Street and then you don't know where to look there's so many windows and roof-tops and parked vehicles maybe ticking away. The corporal shouting, Keep your eyes skinned — I don't want a bullet up me backside because you lot are too busy chatting up the local talent. Blimey! I wish I had six eyes.

We're watching, we're waiting. It's all been planned. The lorry's there and it'll soon be mid-day. The street'll be crowded, pretty busy already. Want some tea? We'll make a noise that'll shake more than this little street: we'll make ourselves known and felt. Ham roll? Ta. Of course people get hurt. But you fight for what you believe in or you're nothing — right? It's the price you have to pay. Watch the lorry . . . .

As the lad and the driver turn the corner, there's a couple of soldiers casually patrolling. The man spins back out of sight, the lad following. They'll check the lorry, note its number — trace him! But if they go back and start unloading . . . .

Then, between them and the lorry, a straggling group of country shoppers emerges from the side road to the High Street car park and makes its way towards the supermarket. The driver pushes through, annoying the old dears and knocking into an old man. There are angry shouts as the driver breaks into a run. The lad looks back at the soldiers turning the corner.

We're watching, we're waiting. Nearly time. Got everything? Let's move.

The corporal shouts, Check that lorry.

The old man is helped to his feet.

The driver opens his cab door and then sees the soldiers running towards him. The crowd scatters.

The lad runs to the telephone box and dials.

The driver drops down and races off up the road, his belly wobbling, his face grey and gasping.

Explosion.

The driver bursts into the neat little house and crouches, sobbing for breath, on the floor. His wife pushes the kids off next door and tries to comfort him.

Outside the supermarket, outside a blazing ruin of wood and glass and bargain offers, lie a few country shoppers, a lorry driver's young mate and a careful corporal.

22   True to life

A comedy in seven scenes

Cast   Martin
        Mrs Smythe — his mother
        Mrs Iggs — his landlady
        Madame Brie — manageress of the Hôtel Superbe, Paris
        Marie ⎫
        Sophie ⎭ waitresses
        Cécile — a scatty, half-deaf chambermaid
        Sir Rich-Patrick — owner of the Hôtel Superbe
        Paul — Martin's friend
        Anna — Paul's sister

Action *Scene one: Mrs Iggs's lodging house, London*
        Mrs Iggs leads Mrs Smythe up the stairs.

MRS IGGS Hoh, yus, 'e's a luverly lad that son o' yours, Missus.
    Never gives me a bit o' bovver, 'e don't. Bet you're right proud
    o' 'im, ain't yer?

MRS SMYTHE (*breathless*) Is it — is it much further?

MRS IGGS Yus, an' 'e speaks so nice, don't 'e? Not la-di-dah I don't
    mean, but proper like, like on the News on telly. Mind you, I
    know the trouble some kids get into — not like 'im, of course, 'e
    knows 'ow to behave, you've brought 'im up right, Missus, I'll
    say that much for you — but take mine —

MRS SMYTHE Are there any more stairs? I think I'm going to have a
    heart attack!

MRS IGGS 'Ad twelve I did, all boys except three, gave me 'ell they
    did. Mind you, they 'aven't done too bad, though I says it as
    shouldn't. There's Mike, me eldest, couldn't keep 'is 'ands off
    nothin', always in trouble. Well, 'e's out now an' got a nice
    little job as a Security Guard. And little Stevie, love 'im, not
    much bigger than me knee when 'e was sixteen, do anythin' with
    a tricycle. Star attraction in the Circus now, hoh yus. And
    Sharon, did I tell you about 'er? Oh, she was a madam, she was!
    After all the boys — out she'd go, lipstick up to her ears, down
    the Disco 'alf the night — an' she were no more than ten then. I

needn't tell you what 'appened, need I — hoh yus.

She knocks on a door and flings it open.

MRS IGGS Martin! Yer mum's 'ere to see you. (*To Mrs Smythe*) I'll see you later, luv, and we'll 'ave a cup o' tea an' a nice chat, eh? Oh yus. (*She goes.*)

MARTIN What are you doing here, Mum? Why didn't you tell me you were coming?

MRS SMYTHE Let me sit down a minute. Whew! I don't know whether it's the stairs or that woman's voice, but I'm worn out, absolutely shattered.

MARTIN I was just making some tea. Like a cup?

MRS SMYTHE I need something. I've got to see *her* on the way down.

MARTIN She's not so bad. Looks after me like one of her own.

MRS SMYTHE Huh! That'll be a lot, I'm sure.

MARTIN Well, is everything all right?

MRS SMYTHE I'm all right. It's *you* I'm worried about — living here like this.

MARTIN Oh, it's OK. Don't worry. I can manage. Social security money covers the rent and food — just about.

MRS SMYTHE 'Just about'. Look at it. And when I think of your lovely home and how your poor father and I worked to keep you properly fed and nicely dressed. Oh. Is that tea ready yet?

Martin pours it out and gives his mother a cup.

MARTIN Well, I know it's not much, but I can work here — and no one bothers me.

MRS SMYTHE Oh, well I'll go if I'm in your way . . . . (*She sniffs.*)

MARTIN I didn't mean it like that. I just want to be an artist, that's all. I just want to try on my own to see if I'm any good.

MRS SMYTHE I'm on my own (*sniff*). Ever since your dear father (*sniff*) passed away (*sniff*) and you left home (*sniff, sniff*) and came to this awful place (*very loud sniffs*), I've been on my own. (*One last loud sniff and she stops.*) So — I'll tell you why I'm here. I want you to come home, Martin, and settle down to a good sensible job. I've kept your little room all ready for you and there'll be a proper hot meal waiting for you when you get home from work. I'll help you pack.

MARTIN It's OK. I'm packed.

MRS SMYTHE You're coming home! How lovely!

MARTIN I'm —

MRS SMYTHE I knew you'd come to your senses sooner or later.

MARTIN I'm going to Paris.

MRS SMYTHE Where?

MARTIN Paris. Tomorrow morning on the ferry.

MRS SMYTHE You mean abroad?

MARTIN Yes, Mum, abroad. But it's not far.

MRS SMYTHE I'll never see you again! My poor little boy!

MARTIN It's not the other side of the moon.

MRS SMYTHE Oh! And there's all those people there.

MARTIN What people?

MRS SMYTHE French. French people. You know what they're like.

MARTIN No, I don't. Not yet. Look, it's where all the artists are. I can get experience.

MRS SMYTHE Oh, yes. You'll get that, all right.

MARTIN I expect I'll become famous.

MRS SMYTHE Yes — but what for?

Scene two: A small boarding house, the Hôtel Superbe, in Paris.

MARTIN Hullo. Can I have your cheapest room, please?

MADAME Our rooms are not cheap, sir.

MARTIN I don't mind what it's like.

MADAME This is a high class hotel.

MARTIN Is it? A young artist called Paul told me to come here.

MADAME Are you an artist? Well, that is different. Perhaps we can find you something not too expensive. Cécile —! (*She waits impatiently for Cécile to appear.*) You can't get the staff nowadays. Cécile — you old fool!

CÉCILE (*appearing, out of breath*) Coming, Madame.

MADAME Follow me. Bring the gentleman's case, Cécile.

CÉCILE Yes, Madame. (*She staggers along behind them.*)

MADAME Up these stairs. Hurry, Cécile.

CÉCILE Yes, Madame. Coming, Madame.

MARTIN Is it very far?

MADAME There are only three hundred and ninety-four steps, sir. Hurry up, Cécile — fool!

CÉCILE Coming, Madame.

A well-dressed man pushes them out of the way to get by.

SIR RICH-PATRICK Out of my way, you ninnies!

CÉCILE Sorry, sir. Coming, Madame.

MARTIN Who was that?

MADAME The owner. He's Sir Rich-Patrick. Lives here when he's in town. Cécile!

CÉCILE Yes, Madame.

MADAME Open the door, fool.

CÉCILE Yes, Madame.

MARTIN What's this? The broom cupboard?

MADAME All you need. A bed, a table, a chair.

MARTIN And a rat. (*A large brown rat scuttles away.*)

MADAME Quite friendly.

CÉCILE Except when they're hungry.

MADAME Shut up, Cécile. You have too much to say. Just feed them twice a day.

MARTIN I'm lucky to get fed that often myself.

MADAME Dinner's at seven. Please sit at the small table.

MARTIN Why?

CÉCILE To get the cheapest food.

Madame frowns.

CÉCILE Yes, Madame.

MARTIN I'm not sure I like it.

MADAME Look at the beautiful wallpaper.

MARTIN In places. What about that? There's a hole in the roof!

MADAME No extra charge for showers, sir. Come, Cécile, you have work to do.

CÉCILE Yes, Madame. (*They leave.*)

Scene three: Kitchen and dining room

MADAME Stir the soup.

CÉCILE Yes, Madame.

MADAME Watch the oven.

CÉCILE Yes, Madame.

SIR RICH-PATRICK (*coming in and sitting down*) I'm here, I'm waiting.

MADAME Thank you, sir. With you immediately. (*To Cécile*) Hurry, fool!

Martin comes in and sits at small table.

MADAME Sophie! Marie!

SOPHIE ⌉Yes, Madame. Coming, Madame! (*They run in and pick up*
MARIE ⌊*trays of dishes and plates.*)

MADAME Now, Sophie, that's for Sir Rich-Patrick.

SOPHIE Yes, Madame. (*She goes to table.*)

MADAME Marie, that's for him — the artist.

MARIE Yes, Madame. (*She goes to table.*)

SIR RICH-PATRICK Where's me dam' serviette?

SOPHIE (*alarmed*) Oh, sir! (*She runs to get one.*)

MADAME (*watching*) Fool! She'll have to go.

MARTIN May I have some wine, please?

MARIE (*embarrassed*) Oh, sir, you don't get wine at this table.
Would you like some water? (*Runs to get some.*)

MADAME (*watching*) Water! Fool! I must advertise!

SIR RICH-PATRICK Where's me rolls and butter? Am I to starve in
me own hotel?

SOPHIE (*terrified*) Oohh! (*She runs to get them.*)

MADAME (*furious*) Oh! (*She turns on Cécile.*) What are you doing? Cut
the meat properly — you don't have to hack it to death! Oh, fool!

CÉCILE Yes, Madame. It's tough, Madame. (*She looks at Madame
menacingly, holding up the knife*) But I am an expert with a knife . . .
Madame.

SIR RICH-PATRICK You!

Martin looks up.

SIR RICH-PATRICK Yes, you. Artist fellow, I suppose.

MARTIN Yes, sir. That is . . . .

SIR RICH-PATRICK I want me portrait painted. You any good?

MARTIN A por-portrait? Yours, sir?

SIR RICH-PATRICK Can you do it?

MARTIN Why, yes, sir.

SIR RICH-PATRICK I want it true to life. I want everyone to see my
best features —

Sophie and Marie giggle.

SIR RICH-PATRICK — my aristocratic nose . . . ,

SOPHIE (*hushed, to Marie*) It's a hook!

SIR RICH-PATRICK My fine brow . . . .

MARIE (*hushed, to Sophie*) Covered in spots!

SIR RICH-PATRICK My firm, manly chin . . . .

SOPHIE (*hushed, to Marie*) Like an old witch!

SIR RICH-PATRICK My gentle, wise eyes . . . .

MARIE (*hushed, to Sophie*) Like a hungry hawk!

MARTIN (*realising the task*) It'll take several sittings, sir.

SIR RICH-PATRICK And I want it to show my inner qualities: loyalty, generosity, kindness, love . . . .

MARTIN Could be a long job, sir.

Scene four: Martin's room, the next day.

Martin is working on the portrait. Sir Rich-Patrick is posing in a splendid military uniform covered with medals.

MARTIN (*as he works*) Keep still, please. (*Pause.*) Turn this way. (*Pause.*) Head up a little more. Good, that's finished another boil.

SIR RICH-PATRICK Another what?

MARTIN (*hastily*) Another royal – royal blue. The tube's empty.

SIR RICH-PATRICK Can I see how it's going?

MARTIN No, this part's very difficult.

SIR RICH-PATRICK What's that?

MARTIN Your nose. It needs a lot of work on it – more red, I think . . . .

SIR RICH-PATRICK Red? For my nose?

MARTIN . . . Mixed with white for a pure skin colour. And the shape – a few more humps and that lump at the end . . . .

SIR RICH-PATRICK Are you talking about me?

MARTIN Oh, no, I'm doing a quick sketch of that rat over there.

SIR RICH-PATRICK (*with a faint shriek*) A rat!

MARTIN It's all right. He's not hungry. He's just finished my socks. Very strong stomachs, rats have. That one's Fred, very friendly.

Paul and Anna come in.

PAUL Hullo, Martin.

MARTIN Hullo, Paul. Hullo, Anna.

ANNA Hullo. Hope you don't mind us dropping in when you're working.

MARTIN Oh, no. Nothing important.

SIR RICH-PATRICK What!

MARTIN I mean, you had nothing important to do today, Anna. You've brought some wine — that's good.

PAUL Let's drink to your new portrait — and fame! Will you have a glass, Sir Rich-Patrick?

SIR RICH-PATRICK Did you buy it here?

PAUL No.

SIR RICH-PATRICK All right, then. Pour me a glass.

Paul pours the wine.

ANNA What's this, Martin?

Paul hands round the wine.

MARTIN (*hushed, as Sir Rich-Patrick drinks*) It's him, Sir Rich-Patrick.

ANNA Martin — it's revolting.

MARTIN Well, it's meant to be true to life.

ANNA Is he paying you for it?

MARTIN Of course. I get a fee for each sitting and a lot more when it's finished.

ANNA Has he seen it yet?

PAUL I wish *I* hadn't.

MARTIN An artist must be true to life . . .

PAUL Oh yes — and starve.

MARTIN What do you mean?

PAUL Don't you see? He won't pay you a penny when he sees that.

ANNA You could make him look a bit nicer.

MARTIN (*looking at Sir Rich-Patrick*) How?

ANNA Well, couldn't you leave out some of those red and yellow bits?

PAUL And you don't have to put in every lump and bump.

SIR RICH-PATRICK Speak up! (*Help himself to more wine.*) Have you finished admiring my portrait? I must go. I have to evict a couple of families this morning, the scoundrels! Can I look?

All three quickly bar his way and edge him towards the door.

ANNA Oh, sir, wait, it's still wet.

PAUL Keep it as a surprise!

MARTIN I want you to see it at its best, sir, when it's done.

SIR RICH-PATRICK Well, all right — but I expect perfection!

PAUL Of course, sir, so you should! 'Bye!

Sir Rich-Patrick goes. They burst into laughter.

Scene five: Martin's room, the next day.
Martin is working on Sir Rich-Patrick's portrait. A large brown rat is watching.

MARTIN Sit still. Head up. Nose this way. You're the best sitter I've ever had, Fred. Better than Sir Rich-Patrick. In fact you're better looking than he is. With you as a model I can go on working when he's not here. The same beady little eyes. (*Works on picture.*) I'll make his a bit narrower than yours – that's it. And the teeth – oh, yours are nice and white. I shall need some black for the cavities – oh yes! Nicely crooked and rotten. There! He'll be proud of that. A spitting image of a fat, rich, money-grabbing, sweaty, rotten, rude, arrogant, ill-mannered brute! A triumph of true art! Thanks, Fred.

Sir Rich-Patrick hurries in. He sees the picture.

SIR RICH-PATRICK Ah, there you are. My God, what's that!

MARTIN Oh it's um – a thingy for . . . er . . . um

SIR RICH-PATRICK You're making about as much sense as that! (*He jabs his finger at the picture.*) I demand to know! Is that supposed to be my portrait? Well, is it?

MARTIN Well, a bit . . . .

SIR RICH-PATRICK A bit? A bit? Which bit? It's a monster!

MARTIN Yes, I know . . . .

SIR RICH-PATRICK It looks – it looks just like a rat!

MARTIN Well, I was working on my sketch of Fred – and I suppose I just got carried away . . .

SIR RICH-PATRICK Carried away! You deserve to be put away! I'm not paying for a thing like that.

MARTIN But you wanted –

SIR RICH-PATRICK I know what I want. People think I'm some kind of a monster –

MARTIN Oh no.

SIR RICH-PATRICK What's that, then? That's what you really think of me.

MARTIN No – it's a mistake.

SIR RICH-PATRICK Liar. You can't even speak the truth, let alone paint it.

MARTIN But that's what I was trying to do.

SIR RICH-PATRICK Fool! Can't you see any more than clothes or size or face? Do you think that's like me because you paint in every blemish and mark? Is every hunchback and cripple a monster? Does a thief have to be ugly?

MARTIN I don't know, I suppose not.

SIR RICH-PATRICK And you! You may be young and clever but that doesn't stop you from being a liar and a cheat.

MARTIN I don't cheat.

SIR RICH-PATRICK You take money for work you can't do. That's cheating. And you're a liar because you haven't the guts to say you meant that to look like me.

MARTIN What shall I do with it?

SIR RICH-PATRICK (going) Give it to Fred – it belongs to him. Goodbye.

Scene six: Martin's room, a few days later.
Martin is working. Madame comes in followed by Cécile.

MADAME Good morning, sir.

MARTIN (gloomily) Morning, Madame.

CÉCILE (looking at picture) Oh sir, how lovely! So handsome!

MADAME (glancing at it) Hmm. There's a faint likeness, I suppose.

CÉCILE Oohh, it's lovely!

MADAME Shut up, Cécile.

CÉCILE Yes, Madame.

MADAME We've had a telephone call from the station. Your mother's on her way here.

MARTIN My mother! What's she doing here?

MADAME I suppose she wants to see you.

MARTIN Oh, all right, thanks.

Anna comes in.

MARTIN Hullo, Anna.

ANNA Hullo. Am I in the way?

MADAME We are just leaving. Come, Cécile.

CÉCILE (looking romantically at them) Oh la-la!

MADAME Cécile!

CÉCILE Yes, Madame. (They go.)

ANNA Martin – how are you? Oh, you do look miserable.

MARTIN I am. Look at this.

She looks at the picture.

ANNA Is that – him?

Martin nods.

ANNA Where's his nose?
MARTIN That delicate little pink blob there.
ANNA What about his big fat stomach?
MARTIN Been on a diet.
ANNA Don't be silly. You've made it look . . . .
MARTIN What?
ANNA Nothing like him.
MARTIN He wanted to be painted like that!
ANNA I preferred the rat picture! Looked more like him anyway.
MARTIN Look – he pays – he gets what he wants.

Anna looks upset.

MARTIN I'm sorry, Anna. What does it matter?
ANNA You know it matters.
MARTIN Yes.
ANNA I haven't seen you for days.
MARTIN I had to start all over again. He didn't want the other
    picture. Why didn't you come to see me?
ANNA (*mysteriously*) I – I've been away.
MARTIN Oh? (*Pause*) By yourself?
ANNA (*teasingly*) No . . . with a . . . someone I know.
MARTIN Who?
ANNA (*laughing*) Why do you want to know?
MARTIN I don't. Stop fooling about, Anna.

Anna laughs.

MARTIN You're just having me on – aren't you?

She shakes her head.

MARTIN (*laughing*) Well, what's so funny, then?
ANNA You are! You're so serious! And jealous!
MARTIN I'm not!
ANNA I went with my brother Paul. That's who!

MARTIN What!

Anna laughs at his look of surprise and relief.

MARTIN I thought . . . .

ANNA I know! Listen, I must tell you. We went to see a friend of
  Paul's in this little village — it's about an hour out of Paris —
  and guess who lives there?

MARTIN Who?

ANNA Sir Rich-Patrick!

MARTIN Oh, him.

ANNA He sort of runs the village, owns just about everything.

MARTIN He would. What did you expect?

ANNA Ah! Well, *not* what they said about him. They like him!

MARTIN (*pointing at his picture*) Him?

ANNA They love him! He does everything for them. Fixes their
  houses, gets them new farm machinery and pays the best wages
  in the district. It's true — he does!

MARTIN You're sure?

ANNA Yes. Oh, they weren't just saying it to protect themselves if
  you're thinking that. No, you can tell when people are telling the
  truth and when they're lying.

MARTIN (*bitterly*) Yes, you can. Well, some people can. *He* can, for
  one. Yes . . . *that* was surprising. I had this mental picture of
  him as some kind of rich money-monster. So that's how I
  painted him. And he called me a liar and a cheat.

ANNA That's not true! Why did he say that?

MARTIN You saw the rat picture, didn't you? And look at this
  rubbish — that's not true, either!

ANNA No . . . he's a sort of mixture of the two.

MARTIN Anna, he can't be both — he can't be a rat *and* a chocolate-
  box hero, can he?

ANNA That's not what I mean. Look, anyone would *think* he was
  just a nasty money-bags — he's so bossy and rude.

MARTIN And he evicts people, don't forget that.

ANNA No he doesn't. Not good people anyway. I heard about those
  two families in the village. They hadn't been there long and no
  one liked them. They were just crooks and swindlers.

MARTIN That's what I thought *he* was!

ANNA And he isn't. He's good and kind.

MARTIN Well why does he make such a secret of it?

ANNA I don't know. But he could hardly come up to you and say, Look, I want to tell how I look after all my village people. Not everyone boasts about what they do.

MARTIN But he wanted this beautiful picture of himself. He told me. He told me exactly how he wanted to look . . .

ANNA You said you were an artist.

MARTIN Yes?

ANNA He thought you would understand.

Martin's mother puffs her way in. She sees Anna.

MRS SMYTHE Oh my God! A woman in his room! (*She faints*)

Scene seven: Sir Rich-Patrick's home. It is several days later.
A small curtain conceals the picture of Sir Rich-Patrick at the end of the room. Long tables are set out for the buffet meal.

MARTIN Anna, you tell her.

ANNA Don't be such a coward. She won't eat you.

MARTIN She still treats me like a baby.

ANNA Then don't be one. Here she comes.

Mrs Smythe rushes in wearing a flamboyant dress and several rows of large pearls. She is very happy.

MRS SMYTHE Oh, it's a dream! Everything's so beautiful – such taste!

MARTIN Mother . . . .

MRS SMYTHE And Sir Rich-Patrick, he's such a dear! And he treats one as a lady should be treated. Charming, absolutely charming!

MARTIN (*nudged by Anna*) Oh, mother . . . we . . . I want to . . .

MRS SMYTHE Later, later, sweet child. There's so much to do! All the village people will be here after the unveiling. So it must be perfect – oh, where's that Madame woman? She hasn't started on the tables yet! (*Rushes off.*)

MARTIN Another failure.

ANNA Don't be silly. And there's no need to worry about your picture – everyone will like it.

MARTIN Except him. And then I won't get paid. And then we can't get married.

ANNA Shut up, Martin, you don't get out of it as easily as that!

Madame sweeps in angrily followed by Sophie, Marie and Cécile all bearing heavy trays of food and drink.

MADAME Come along, come along, come along! That woman! Intruder! Stealing his affections! Ordering me about! Cécile — we haven't all day!

CÉCILE Yes, Madame.

MADAME All this waste! What's got into the man? Sophie, another tray — quickly!

SOPHIE Yes, Madame. (*She runs out, and returns with a tray.*)

MADAME It's that woman — she's turned his brain. (*Imitating.*) 'Oh, Sir Rich-Patrick! How wonderful, Sir Rich-Patrick!' Oh, I know *her* sort! After his money, without a doubt!

Paul comes in, to the obvious delight of Sophie and Marie.

PAUL (*to Anna and Martin*) Hullo! When am I to be best man then? (*He sees their faces.*) Hasn't St George fought the dragon yet? (*To Martin, in a joking half-whisper.*) Well, I wouldn't blame you if you've changed your mind about marrying her!

His sister aims a blow at him. He darts away to Sophie and Marie.

PAUL Ladies. (*He bows.*) May I present — (*He produces two bunches of flowers from behind his back. They take them, giggling.*)

SOPHIE } Oh, sir! Ooohh!
MARIE

MADAME Girls! There are more trays in the kitchen. Hurry up!

Sophie and Marie run out happily as Mrs Smythe returns.

MADAME Ahh, Mrs Smythe?

MRS SMYTHE Yes? Quick, quick, I'm busy!

MADAME I should warn you —

MRS SMYTHE Warn me? What's wrong?

MADAME You are — to stay here. With Sir Rich-Patrick. He is — oh, I must say it — a dangerous man. Yes! very dangerous.

Cécile stops work to listen.

MRS SMYTHE Oh!

MADAME Yes, the dreadful stories I could tell! Such scandal — such women! You should return to England immediately!

CÉCILE (*approaching with knife*) Madame . . .

MADAME (*with a shriek*) Cécile! Put that knife down at once!

CÉCILE (*nearer*) You think I'm a silly old fool — (*jabs with knife*) — don't you, Madame?

MADAME No . . .!

CÉCILE You treat me like dirt — (*jabs again*) — under your feet.

MADAME I don't . . . I don't . . .

CÉCILE You have no love — no respect! (*A jab — a shriek.*) And now you are telling lies — lies! — to this good lady. Yes? Yes!

MADAME (*cowering away*) Yes!

As Cécile raises her knife, Madame gives a howl and dashes out.

MARTIN (*going to his mother*) Are you all right? Sit down.

MRS SMYTHE (*sitting*) Oh dear! What a dreadful woman!

Cécile brings her a glass of wine.

MRS SMYTHE Oh thank you, my dear — you were so good to help me.

They all thank Cécile, to her great embarrassment.

CÉCILE (*covering her ears*) No, no, please. *You* are good, English lady. *She* is — (*She draws her finger across her throat.*)

Sir Rich-Patrick comes in followed by Sophie and Marie still fluttering and giggling.

SIR RICH-PATRICK Ah, Millicent, my dear! Here you are — as busy as ever, as lovely as ever!

The maids giggle loudly.

SIR RICH-PATRICK Now to business — and pleasure, I hope. Draw the curtain, Cécile.

She does so to a chorus of Ahhs and Ohhs. The painting is an abstract — two lines cross on a red background and there is a large white rose-shaped blob near the bottom.

PAUL (*quickly*) Brilliant! Most exciting!

SIR RICH-PATRICK (*quietly*) Very . . . clever. (*He smiles at Martin*) Millicent, what do you think of it?

MRS SMYTHE Well, Arthur, now that I know you . . . better . . . I can see it's really quite like you — like a brave knight carrying a white rose — I think that's meant to be a rose — for his lady-love.

SIR RICH-PATRICK Wonderful, wonderful! You understand perfectly, my dear. Martin, you clever scoundrel . . . .

MARTIN (*anxiously*) What?

SIR RICH-PATRICK Sold!

ANNA We can get married!

MRS SMYTHE (*looking at them*) Of course — and about time, too. I thought you were never going to make up your minds.

SIR RICH-PATRICK Perhaps, Millicent, I can be a bit quicker. I've made up my mind. (*He takes her hands.*) What about you?

MRS SMYTHE Oh yes! I made up my mind as soon as I saw your portrait. Where did I put it, Cécile?

Cécile finds a wrapped painting in the corner. She hands it to Mrs Smythe, who unwraps it.

MARTIN (*with a groan*) The rat picture!

SIR RICH-PATRICK Why is that here? Do you like it?

MRS SMYTHE It doesn't do you justice, of course, Arthur — but there's something so lovable and friendly about it. It's so true to life.

MARTIN (*half-choking*) Fred!

Sir Rich-Patrick roars with laughter and delight. Cécile offers drinks and they lift their glasses to the two pictures.

Players and the play Of course many plays aren't true to life. They are about people who are not like anyone you ever meet, and extraordinary things happen to them. But we are convinced long enough to believe what is happening to the characters. Some plays are more like real life. Audiences believe in the characters in long-running serials or 'soap-operas' — they actually send them Get Well cards or flowers if they fall ill or die. At the same time they know that Coronation Street and Ambridge don't exist — except in their imagination. The characters become real to us as we follow their lives, so that it matters what happens to them.

In the play 'True to life' we see the main character from various exaggerated points of view, intended for comic effect. At first he is unbelievable and not true to life, like his portrait. He is seen as a monster and as a chocolate box hero, but as we get to know him he becomes more like life, more human. And the people around him, the painter, his mother, Madame, Cécile, Anna, at last show their own human feelings. The play's final message is to find the truth in our own lives by understanding the simple fact that we are human beings.

Writing and discussion

- Do you prefer plays which are true to life or those which exaggerate people and events?
- Describe your favourite soap-opera. Is it true to life?
- Describe the most unconvincing stage set you've seen. Did it matter that it was unconvincing?
- What is the final message of the play for you?
- What fictional place or character you came across in childhood did you most believe in?
- Describe the most realistic play you've seen.

ACKNOWLEDGEMENTS

We are grateful to the following for permission to reproduce copyright material:

the author's agents for an extract from *The Lark* by Jean Anouilh, translated by Christopher Fry; Heinemann Educational Books for permission to base 'Love is all' on the story *Ginger and Sharon* by P. Abbs; the author, N. F. Simpson for extracts from *The Cresta Run*; University of Minnesota Press for extracts from 'The Caucasian Chalk Circle' in *Parables for the Theatre: Two Plays* by Bertolt Brecht, Eric and Maja Bentley, translators. Copyright © 1948 by Eric Bentley.